George Clayton Johnson— FICTIONEER

~

from *Ocean's Eleven*,
through *The Twilight Zone*,
to *Logan's Run*

BY
VIVIEN COOPER

GEORGE CLAYTON JOHNSON—FICTIONEER
FROM *OCEAN'S ELEVEN*, THROUGH
THE TWILIGHT ZONE, TO *LOGAN'S RUN*
©2013 VIVIEN COOPER

ALL RIGHTS RESERVED.

No part of this book may be reproduced in any form or by any means, electronic, mechanical, digital, photocopying, or recording, except for in the inclusion of a review, without permission in writing from the publisher.

Published in the USA by:

BEARMANOR MEDIA
P.O. BOX 71426
ALBANY, GEORGIA 31708
www.BearManorMedia.com

ISBN-10: 1-59393-736-9 (alk. paper)
ISBN-13: 978-1-59393-736-2 (alk. paper)

COVER IMAGE: Photographer Mark Lampert,
From the Boneyard Collection, Director/Writer Edward L. Plumb.

DESIGN AND LAYOUT: VALERIE THOMPSON

Table of Contents

A Note to the Reader . . . 1

Introduction . . . 3

1929 . . . 7

The Prairie . . . 11

Liberty . . . 15

Camaraderie . . . 19

Peril . . . 23

Discernment . . . 27

Imprisonment . . . 29

Disillusionment . . . 33

Monsters . . . 35

Adjustment . . . 41

Imagination . . . 47

Cinema . . . 51

Change . . . 57

Tragedy . . . 63

Alienation . . . 67

The Orphanage . . . 69

Independence . . . 73

Transition . . . 79

Clarity . . . 83

Photo Album . . . 85

Jack Russell . . . 107

LOVE . . . 111

MARRIAGE . . . 115

HOME . . . 117

STRUGGLE . . . 121

OCEAN'S ELEVEN . . . 123

THE GROUP . . . 129

ALL OF US ARE DYING . . . 133

EXECUTION . . . 135

COMPANIONSHIP . . . 139

CONVENTIONS . . . 141

FICTIONEERS . . . 145

RAY BRADBURY . . . 147

STAR TREK . . . 149

ROUTE 66 . . . 151

LEVERAGE . . . 153

A PENNY FOR YOUR THOUGHTS . . . 155

THE PRIME MOVER . . . 157

A GAME OF POOL . . . 161

KICK THE CAN . . . 165

LOGAN'S RUN . . . 167

NOTHING IN THE DARK . . . 173

NINETY YEARS WITHOUT SLUMBERING . . . 177

IDENTIFICATION . . . 181

UNITY . . . 183

AFTERWORD . . . 187

ACKNOWLEDGMENTS . . . 189

ABOUT THE AUTHOR . . . 191

INDEX . . . 193

~ A Note to the Reader ~

My dear friend and mentor, George Clayton Johnson, was born in 1929. In 2004, I began interviewing him for this book—a labor of love. He was almost seventy-five years old when we began. During the ensuing eight years, I spoke to George almost every Wednesday (think *Tuesdays with Morrie**).

What follows is a portrait of George's life, as remembered by George and written by me…but it is more than that. It is a journey through some of the pivotal events that shaped the early days of television and film.

Rewind to my own youth, when I was led onto a set at Universal Studios by my special-effects-technician father, Larry Needham. Dad knew how much I loved Rod Serling, so he made special arrangements for me to spend some time with him. God bless Dad.

As I marveled over being face to face with Rod Serling, I had no idea that life would one day bring me full-circle, introducing me to George, one of the writers of *The Twilight Zone*, and leading me once again into another dimension.

So, if you will, join me now at twilight time as one of the world's master storytellers materializes upon the screens of our imaginations and relates a lost episode of American life. Or, as Rod Serling might say, "Consider, if you will…"

* For simplicity's sake, titles of all kinds in this book are italicized.

~ Introduction ~

In many ways, the landscape of our country bears so little resemblance to the America of the 1930s that, had you tried to describe it then to the young George Clayton Johnson, it might have seemed the fantastical and wild imagining of a mind just a little bit mad. Like a tale distilled from the genius of our storyteller, himself…There's no doubt about it: life in this digital age seems to have been drawn right from an episode of *The Twilight Zone*—an episode where media is king.

Those first television sets, over which shows like *The Twilight Zone* were broadcast, were initially beheld with awe and a kind of humble reverence. But, we have since grown suspicious. Once seen as welcome guests in our homes—novel, mysterious and solicitous—TV and the much more complex and sophisticated devices which have followed, have permanently insinuated themselves into every corner of our lives.

Those early TV sets were charming, hand-crafted wood cabinets, pretending false modesty and ignorance. They stuck rabbit ears on their heads to give themselves the appearance of innocence, and us the illusion of control. As if *we* could adjust *them*. As if we could turn them off and on.

Now, our TV's, iPads, iPods, Smart Phones, and other media delivery devices are everywhere. The media of today is not your father's television set and it will not be ignored. And despite all our protests to the contrary, we wouldn't have it any other way.

Our media devices have so long been like members of the family that it is easy to forget those days when inviting a TV over the threshold and into the living room was like opening the door to

Martians. No one knew what to expect. And while these devices have far exceeded our expectations, it is easy to wonder why we ever answered the door in the first place.

But if we pause—and pause we can, at will, thanks to our DVR boxes—we will remember...

In the beginning, television was a mystic, a prophet, a prescient, unassuming Native American with his ear to the ground, ready to point the way, ready to chart our course and forecast the weather for the journey. It suggested our destination and grooved new roads, allowing us to get there faster and wind up places we'd only dreamed. And in those days, when we were still inviting the neighbors in to marvel over the newfangled contraption, television still walked softly and carried a big stick.

Today, subtlety and innuendo are casualties of the information age and we are fed a steady diet of blatant images, and hit over the head with overt violence and sexuality. Television is more provocative than ever, but that doesn't mean it always provokes deep thought and reflection.

But it wasn't always this way. Shows like *The Twilight Zone* and *Kung Fu*, for which George Clayton Johnson wrote episodes, posed the question, "What if?"

What if there was a device that could pick you up, toss you over its shoulder, carry you into the most remote galaxy—and later that same night, retrieve you, wrap you in buffalo skin, and deposit you in the middle of the American wilderness to sleep off your bizarre odyssey?

What if, with a flick of the wrist, we could pull the thread and tear the seams between this world and the next...if we could slip behind the veil that separates the dimensions...if the edges of the little boxes we live and work in are nothing but cardboard flaps, waiting to be lifted to reveal entire universes beyond our comprehension?

What if a man could crawl in and out of the television set at his whim, being simultaneously the storyteller, an ancient character of his own invention, and a flesh and blood incarnation of television, itself, moving about in this futuristic today?

Meet George Clayton Johnson. We cannot speak of him without talking about television and film. His life's breath, his fingerprints, his very DNA are embedded in the world of story making for the screen (small and large), just as the imprint of that media is imbedded in his very essence. What we think of as the classic episodic story, as the blueprint and the embryo for everything that was later spawned, is a product of storytellers like George Clayton Johnson and his colleagues.

Like the American Indian in an old television show who sits quietly against the side of the saloon with the secret upon which everything depends; like the gunslinger hero who slips noiselessly down the dusted pathway that cuts through the middle of town, measuring his steps and choosing the moment he will make his critical move; like the everyman who sits in an overstuffed chair in his living room and discusses with his wife what should be done in light of the fact that it is indeed the last evening of civilization as we know it, George Clayton Johnson is both an extraordinary character in the center of an eerily ordinary world and an ordinary man in an extraordinary environment.

A Penny for Your Thoughts, Execution, The Prime Mover, Nothing in the Dark, Kick the Can, A Game of Pool, All of Us Are Dying, and *Ninety Years Without Slumbering*—these *Twilight Zone* stories penned by Johnson, along with countless others written by his contemporaries, gave birth to an entire genre of storytelling, television, and movie making.

Kung Fu, the premiere episode of *Star Trek, Honey West, Route 66, The Law* and *Mr. Jones. Logan's Run. Ocean's Eleven.* The list of Johnson's television, film and literary credits is a spool of film that goes on for hours. Be it a literary story, teleplay or screenplay, the art and game of the story is the same; the screen just grows or shrinks, depending.

Just as *The Twilight Zone* was a marriage of the mundane and the fantastical, defying classic science-fiction stereotyping, George himself is a compilation. A hybrid. A composite character. In the snapshots of his life that are about to unfold, you will find preserved timeless nuggets of Twentieth-Century American life, as played out in real time in the life of a certain man who became George Clayton Johnson, Fictioneer.

His story gives us glimpses into the mental, emotional, and spiritual terrain where some of our favorite stories for television and film were hatched, and then projected onto a screen with the time code running.

Ultimately, this is a tale not only about a man, a storyteller, and a complex character, but about us all. When we pull shut the doors of our workplace in the evening, and make our way home to our television sets, when we burrow into our couch cushions to watch TV, who is watching whom? Who is controlling whom? Is television reflecting us, or are we reflecting television? Where do any of our lives begin and end? Where does television start and then leave off?

As Rod Serling would warn as we entered *The Twilight Zone*, "You are about to enter another dimension, a dimension not only of sight and sound but of mind…"

Yes. Sight, sound, and ultimately mind. For that is where the journey always begins. In a world where reality television has created in us an unnatural appetite for voyeuristic spectacle, and thereby commandeered the airwaves, the craft and genius of concocting a story in the vast regions of one's mind is becoming a lost art. And no one knows that better than George Clayton Johnson.

~ 1929 ~

> "…She comes up to him. 'I've had time to think. I'm sorry for the way I acted. I was frightened.'
> *'But you're not frightened now?'*
> 'Yes, I suppose I am. The idea that someone knows everything you think is a frightening thing. And yet, if you truly care for someone…' Her voice falters.
> *'Hush,' he says. 'I know…'*
> 'It's a wonderful gift,' she says. 'I should appreciate that you have it.'
> *'Wonderful? It's a terrible gift. It's a curse. People think things and don't do them—they do things and don't think them—and worst of all, you discover what people really think of you. It's hideous!…'"*
> (A Penny for Your Thoughts, the story upon which George's teleplay of the same name was based)

As our story opens in January of 1929, a cartoon hero is born who is neither enormous in size nor extraordinary in intellect. It is Popeye the Sailor Man, and he will become famous for his motto, "I am what I am."

One month later, in February, while most men are at the local florist, buying Valentine's Day roses for their wives or girlfriends, seven gangsters rivaling mob boss, Al Capone, are murdered in Chicago, Illinois.

In theaters, movie gangsters will play with great dramatic flair, safely removed from the streets where the blood is actually being spilled. All over America, young men will get ideas about what it means to be a man from movie heroes like Humphrey Bogart and Edward G. Robinson.

While no one can yet put their finger on it, it is also a time when the economy is spinning like a plate on the head of a man walking a tightrope—much like it is today, with the New Millennium in its teen years.

It is against this backdrop that a beauty named Laura Mae Duke (known simply as Mae) and her husband, Charles Edward Johnson, First Sergeant, Fifth Division of the United States Army, begin to see in her growing belly the signs of her pregnancy with their second son.

They will decide to name him George Clayton. He will be born in a barn, one month after Jewish diarist Anne Frank, who will go on to memorialize in writing some of the unspeakable events that will transpire during World War II. In this year of 1929, such things are still beyond the scope of human imagination.

Our hero's birth will occur on July 10th, on the heels of our country's annual fireworks celebration, with the smoke still thick in the air, six days after Independence Day.

By that time, the first ever Academy Awards broadcast will have aired, beginning the national obsession with fame and our adoration of the movie star. Little do Charles and Mae Johnson know, when they look upon the face of their newest bundle, that he will someday write for some of the country's favorite TV shows and movies.

When the boy is four months old, the entire financial world falls like Atlas with a two-by-four to his back. In October of that year, the Great Depression officially begins.

(NOTE TO THE READER: PASSAGES IN ITALICS INDICATE GEORGE SPEAKING.)

It was a fascinating part of the twentieth century, with everything changing by leaps and bounds. Before 1929, everyone was prosperous. Then everything changed, and there was a tremendous amount of poverty. Everyone became poor. It was a whole new world in which those who had money had power to exercise, and those who didn't were little better than sharecroppers—if they even had a share, at all.

Even in my childhood, I had a clear sense of equality, and I couldn't understand why things were the way they were. There were separate bathrooms and the whole back-of-the-bus thing. I was also aware of the wretched state of women. It was a man's world, and women couldn't even open a bank account.

And it is in this era of scarcity, turmoil and financial depression that George Clayton, known simply as Clayton, begins growing up.

My mom and dad were products of the wretched life of the working poor. We had meager food and poor lodging, so you couldn't help but be grateful for everything. You took your shoes off to run barefoot around the prairie. When your shoes wore out, you didn't buy new shoes, you simply put new soles on your shoes. Your shoes couldn't be replaced.

It was out of that poverty that all our manners and mores came. "Use it up, wear it out, make it do or do without." That was the motto of the day. It was a time of extreme frugality, and even as a grown man, those values are imbedded in me. I am a child of the Great Depression and I know how to do without.

Money was so scarce and so important, I rejected its importance. It became part of my character to say, "No, I won't do that. I can do without the money. I will starve first."

Some children had one or two possessions but I had nothing. And yet because everyone was poor, no one was poor. It wasn't even the extreme poverty that we felt—it was the parsimony that went with it. Just as people could be frugal, they could also be incredibly generous. If a family had a dollar and twenty-seven cents between them and death, they would split it with you.

~ The Prairie ~

Amid the rambling prairie land of the mid-1930s, near Cheyenne, Wyoming, lives our young hero. He is now five years old, and this year, right around his birthday, the world is introduced to both Donald Duck and Adolf Hitler, the new Fuhrer of Germany.

This is the landscape of the world—on the one hand sparkling with bright explosions of creativity and imagination, and on the other, simmering with dark intentions and plots more sinister than any movie tale.

It is the year *The Wonderful Wizard of Oz* is purchased by Metro-Goldwyn-Mayer, and *Cleopatra* and *The Thin Man* fill the big screen in movie theaters.

And it is not only a time of great movies. Like hazy silhouettes of spirits not yet fully incarnate, all manner of electronic media are coming to life. Still, the thought that they will someday be as commonplace in our homes as the pillows upon which we lay our heads to sleep at night is a notion fit for a tale of science fiction.

All these opposing forces are at play simultaneously as our young man begins to learn about the world. So, it is not surprising that he will one day engage in the business of "What if?" and help to forge an entire genre of science fiction and fantasy.

For now, life is simple.

Inside his home, we see a big room sparsely furnished with an icebox, a rough table, and simple wooden chairs. Crouching in the center of the room like a small black bear stuffed with food and ready for hibernation is the pot belly stove. This is the main living area and it stands guard before two small sleeping areas. Long before noon, the sun will be hot lava pouring down upon the earth.

For now, the walls are chilled like the edges of a cave, so the distended belly of the stove is glowing blistering hot.

Like warm kittens, the children sleep, contented. Checking on them at night, their mom's breath smells like potent spirits, but the children think no more of it than the smell of wood burning in the stove. Alcohol is simply one of the fragrances that scent their lives. Yes, the offspring of Laura Mae Duke, now known as Mae Johnson, sleep well, in that unencumbered slumber of youth, their young shoulders unburdened.

Five years older and a world of experience removed from Clayton is Charles Edward, Junior, who sometimes lets his younger brother, Clayton, tag along with him.

Ronald Lee, on the other hand, is five years short of Clayton's age, and ten years Charlie's junior. Five years on either side of him, our hero and his brothers are connected by familial love and loyalty, all emptying into the same sea, but as removed from each other's daily activities as the banks of the river of years separating them.

In the middle of these boys is Ramona Mae, only twenty-two months behind our hero, and in her disposition—open, friendly, and sunny—his twin. (A set of twins—Kenneth and Kathleen—will come later, and so will Lola Merle and Judy.)

In harmony, Clayton and Ramona often sing together, and in harmony often accompany each other in life, the nearly two years between them a gap more easily bridged than the five years on either side that he has between him and his brothers. Ramona is often by his side on hikes down to the creek, and always under his wing when endangered by any of the perils of prairie life.

Then, at last, we see the face of our five-year-old hero, his eyelashes brushing his cheek in sleep. He is slight in build, and fair. His light hair is the color of warm moonlight. In the deep lavender of early dawn, his cherubic features are lit by the forgiving glow of a kerosene lamp. And it is this that he will always remember—a world illuminated by kerosene lamps.

That rosy glow from the kerosene lamps cast everything in its best light. It was a form of Heaven for me in those days. There were always exciting things to do, and things were great...

Even-tempered and steady, Father is a constant in the life of his son. Not given to great displays of affection, Clayton's dad nevertheless loves his children in a quiet way. Again and again throughout his life, our boy will return to his father, like a man in the wilderness finding his way back to the lap of a great mountain.

If Father is quiet and sure like a mountain, Mother is mercurial. Unwavering in her love for her children, she is nonetheless a wild wind, at times whipping up in great gusts, and at other times sweet and soft as a gentle breeze. Driven by a longing only she can feel, like the low moan of a coyote on the prairie, she often finds herself drawn into the local bars.

Powdered and painted, she holds court, the sounds of "Everything I Have is Yours" by Rudy Vallee, and "Love In Bloom" by Bing Crosby wailing in the distance.

Already enterprising, our boy is often out peddling newspapers, or finding some other way to put a nickel in his pocket. In his travels, he will come upon his mother in a bar. The two will embrace and she will invite him to join her. As she sits with her compatriots and ruminates upon the incredible changes that have come upon America, Clayton will play at her feet, crawling around under the booth, investigating the peanut machines.

I always felt loved by both of my parents. There was never any question I was my father's kid, and many years later, I would travel great distances to seek him out. He would always point me out to his friends, showing pride in the fact that I was his son.

My mother never spoke down to me. She always spoke to me directly, and made me feel seen and heard. Even if she was spending the day in the bar, I was welcome. She never made me feel rejected or isolated. There was something very romantic about her, like a flapper, and she was nonchalantly independent. She was not just her husband's slave.

~ Liberty ~

As a new day whispers in our young hero's ear and wakes him, he rises swiftly and without dread. His home may be threadbare, and the family's security precarious, but he knows none of this. He has his liberty, and that is enough. He is free.

As the years tumble on and his ankle catches in a time warp, he will be sucked into an internal vortex where he will become intimately familiar with his interior world. While it will eventually liberate him, he will for a long spell, be utterly and completely trapped.

And so liberty, above all else, is to be prized. And even though he cannot possibly see beyond the rolling hills of his early childhood to spy the jailer heading his way, somewhere inside of this carefree, happy little boy is already a deep appreciation for liberty. Unencumbered by the tight leash usually imposed upon children, he runs on a long tether, free to roam and explore.

It is this that tints his world rosy and races his heart. His mind, quick and agile, is always imagining the possibilities of the day, leaping ahead into the enchanted worlds that wait outside his door. And for now, in this time of the mid-1930s, Clayton's entire world exists outside the door.

If we could linger as time turns the boy into an adolescent, we would find shoved into his pockets many papers filled with words written in magic code, maps that lead into secret places inside the mind and soul. Secret places where he is both master and king, where he alone possesses the golden key of entry, and over which he, alone, has dominion. It is an expansive territory where he is not left behind or diminished, where he is not at any disadvantage; where he is never devalued.

Papers and pages filled with words and images. Comic books, pulp magazines, and compact little treasures that will make history as the first paperback books. Books—pieces of parchment that have collected words like buckets catching raindrops. And it is in this bath of words and images that our young man will baptize himself over and over, giving birth to an entire universe of his own creation.

But for today, it is still mid-summer, and Clayton is on a mission.

The opaque yellow sky whitens as the day grows hot. Rushing outside, our young boy knows exactly where he is going and what he is after. Like children before him who have followed the sound of a piccolo into lush forests filled with mystery, Clayton has found a piper, and it is his song that he longs to hear today, and to his doorstep that he is headed.

Charlie Peterson.

Unlike other children, Clayton follows no one blindly, but is guided by a divine hand. He is collecting notes for his own song, and it is from the many tones and textures he will pick up along his journey across time that he will eventually whittle and hone a writing voice, singular and pure.

Charlie is an entire year or two older, a good head taller and beginning to sport muscles that are, as yet, only sketches on the body of our hero. Much as a young boy might capture a beautiful spider under a glass jar and spend hours studying its many furry legs, curious patterns and habits, Clayton is drawn to Charlie and absorbed by him. Magnetized.

Charlie's age, his size, the alien machinations of his mind, so different from the sharp intellect of our boy—all these things meld together to spark Clayton's imagination. Whenever Charlie and Clayton are together, Charlie shares new worlds with Clayton.

The Petersons were wealthy compared to most. They lived in a big home with a garage, a windmill, and a water pump. They even had tools. Imagine digging a pit as big as a house. You have one huge room, and then you get packing boxes and pile them against the wall so there's one endless bookshelf running the length of the house, with orange crate partitions stacked head high to create the illusion of rooms.

I'll never forget walking into their house and seeing, jammed between the orange crates, a piano, and instead of couches, they had a bed in this little alcove. It was all very artful. I thought, my God, they've got a piano! It astonished me. It was a big deal. Only rich people had a piano.

My mother was never surprised when I wanted to go to the Petersons' and hang around with them in the mornings while they drank their coffee. Charlie was my hero in those days and my mother knew how much I loved him, and that going to his house was my daily routine.

Sometimes my mother would come, too, and my sister Ramona, and Ramona and I would be asked to do "our act." They loved how well we could harmonize together, and there was a quality in our singing—the sincerity, the purity—that everyone appreciated. "Go ahead, Clayton, sing! Sing!" The Petersons would be egging us on. And my sister Ramona and I would sing, "Home, home on the range..."

I've always believed that it really is the singer we connect with, much more than the song. Like for me, when I think of great writers I love and I think of their writing, whether I am reading Ray Bradbury or Dashiell Hammett, it is their voice that I'm longing to hear, their voice that resonates with me, and their voice that speaks to my heart, no matter what story I'm reading, or what style or genre. And from the time I was a child, I knew I was born to sing...

A year later, Clayton, at six, will be in a country schoolhouse. He will close his eyes and open his throat to sing, and in his young voice will be heard a prayer of praise. It is the sound of a flute, pure and clear. The name Johnson is halfway through the middle of the alphabet, so by the time he's sung his song, eight or ten other kids will have already taken their turn. But with the others, each one is stopped after a few bars, and surrenders the floor to the next student.

When Clayton sings, it is different. The teacher, and all the other little birds in the school, will be so taken by the sound of his voice, that time will stand suspended and the teacher will forget to stop him so the next student can stand up in turn and sing his three bars.

Clayton will stand straight and tall, his chin tilted towards Heaven, and his voice will be transcendent. The piano will help him carry "*Great God, Our King*" all the way to the end of the line.

As his last note breaks like a branch and falls slowly, the whole classroom will explode in loud applause.

Everyone thought my voice was pure and sweet and that day, my teacher chose me to be the soprano voice for the Christmas program.

Life was wonderful. I had learned to read early, I could sing, and now I was going to have a big part in the Christmas program. For a moment in time, I felt like a star.

~ Camaraderie ~

For now, Clayton is still five years old—but he already understands that it must be in the spirit of humility and appreciation that he accompanies Charlie, an older student of life, on his journey that day. And it is this quality in Clayton—this respect, reverence and humility—that opens the Petersons' door, as it will open doors for him forever.

In fact, Clayton may be a Johnson first and foremost, but he has become an honorary Peterson, able to blend in easily with the Peterson children, to carry himself as they do, to speak as they do and never strike a wrong chord. And so he knocks on their door and hears, as he always does, those wonderful words, "Come in!"

Today, he will spend the morning at their home, and like many days during these years of his life, he will learn to walk and run and play as Clayton and simultaneously inhabit the atmosphere of Charlie Peterson.

The Petersons were very hospitable and I would go home if I was told to, so I never overstayed my welcome. Charlie was everyone's leader and it was because of his enthusiasm that we would follow him. I would wait for him to get around to doing his chores, and then we would take a bucket, pump some water and lug it several blocks into the prairie…

On either end of the broom handle, the pails slosh and dance as the boys carefully coax them along. Charlie and Clayton scan the ground for those earthen mounds that poke out of the dirt like buried sombreros. They are a two-man posse, and their fugitives hear them coming. Burrowed beneath the earth, the colonies of prairie dogs sniff trouble above them and let out a series of shrill whistles.

At the boys' feet are Spud and Drainie Peterson, a white bulldog and a black-and-white border collie who is a born investigator. Drainie knows the difference between a gopher hole and buried treasure and only when he finds evidence of the coveted prairie dogs does he begin to feverishly dig.

Seeing that Drainie has found one, the boys are jumping and hollering and furiously grabbing for their pails. At the precise moment, the boys begin to pour water down the hole of the prairie dog. Gasping, sputtering, coughing, it surfaces—the beautiful prairie dog boasting stripes up and down its back.

We kept a reserve bucket and we would leave it poised in front of the hole in case the drowning creature came struggling out of the hole and waited to see what was going to happen next.

Disoriented and shocked, the prairie dog lingers for just a moment, trying to gauge the source of this deluge. And as impeccably and effortlessly as a Kung Fu student executing a kick, Clayton pounces on the prairie dog as it comes rushing out of the hole and right into his bucket, which he clasps close to his chest.

He has done it—used his understanding of the animal's nature to draw him close. Captured the prize with his wit and speed.

This time it turned out we had caught a mother and several babies. These beautiful little things came struggling up after her. We caught them and put them under our shirts to dry them off. Then, getting them in the sun, they became very frisky...

Working in concert, Charlie and Clayton try to hold the mother prairie dog in a bucket, but frantic and powerful, she is no match for them. Like quicksilver, she is out of there before they can blink.

But there are still the babies. Charlie holds them and Clayton carefully slips a collar fashioned of safety pin and string around their tiny necks. Swee'pea. Dick Tracy. Popeye. And Skeezix. Named after favorite cartoon strips.

Victorious and triumphant, the boys let their little captives loose to run over their shoulders before leading them home on leashes.

We didn't realize at the time how much we'd accomplished when we caught them, but they were so exotic, everyone wanted to see them. It was such an adventure, looking for likely sites, then capturing them, and walking for miles, leading them home.

It was really memorable to be involved in this business—the work of carrying the buckets, the mutual leadership, sharing the adventure, earning the prize, being a part of the hunt that attracts all this attention.

And for our budding writer, these things—the mutual collaboration and shared leadership; the adventure of exploring new terrains within his mind and with his peers; the basic chop-wood-and-carry-water work of crafting a creation; and ultimately the prize of recognition—will always be the ultimate prizes in life.

Many years later, while spending a lot of time trying to make my way as a writer, I will meet another Charles I admire greatly—Charles Beaumont. We will meet at a time when I have learned a lot about how to talk the game rather than do it. Then, my life will change.

~ Peril ~

He is six years old now, a year older than he was on the prairie dog hunt.

In the spring of this year, Adolf Hitler announces rearmament, totally disregarding the Versailles Treaty.

On the big screen, it is a good year for film. Judy Garland signs a contract with M-G-M; *Anna Karenina,* Hitchcock's *The 39 Steps, Les Miserables, Mutiny on the Bounty,* and *A Midsummer Night's Dream* land in theaters.

Our young hero has never been to the movies. Nor does he have any way of knowing that France is beginning to broadcast regular television transmission from the top of the Eiffel Tower, or that this is the year of the first television broadcasts in Germany and England.

"Now, Clayton, don't be too long, dear!" Mae kisses the boy on his forehead, tousles his hair and sends him to the store.

As Clayton starts out the door that late afternoon in mid-summer, Woody Allen and Luciano Pavarotti are lying somewhere in a crib, and Elvis Presley, Carol Burnett and Julie Andrews are also in diapers.

On what promises to be the simplest of errands, Clayton does not linger or take a backwards look at his beloved mother. He rushes outside, never stopping to fill his eyes one last time with the sight of their warm and cozy little home, or to ponder his world that up until this exact moment in time has been so uncomplicated and lovely.

The prairie sky forebodes nothing, not the hint of a storm, and the landscape looks to him as safe as it always has, with nothing out of order. Only it is dusk—that sparkling, silvery blue curtain that falls lightly upon the land and skews the vision.

Our boy does not think twice. It is with the lightest of hearts and the most carefree state of mind that he bounds down the road. He is eager to be off on his adventure to collect supplies from the store for his mother.

It is written that the prince of darkness can be clever indeed, transforming himself as easily into a serpent or a king. And sometimes, too, the good, loving hand of Providence chooses the simplest, most unremarkable tool from the shed. Often, it is hard to say which forces are at work until hindsight provides the answer.

So it is that no one knows the powers at play on this day out of many, when a mere acquaintance, a neighborhood boy, finds himself desirous of a walk, and sets out upon the same path as our young hero, eventually catching up with him.

Roaming around the store, Clayton admires the black licorice and the lemon and horehound drops sold in bulk. The clerk winks and gives him a couple of gumdrops for his pocket. He sets the sack of potatoes down on the wood counter of the small country store, and waits for the clerk to mark off the Johnson account for the amount of the purchase. Then Clayton tucks the bag under his arm, and starts back towards home.

Unaware of the part he is about to play in directing the pieces around on the board of Clayton's life, a neighborhood boy is as surprised as Clayton is when they run into each other. With the unquestioning acceptance of children, the pawn and our hero start together towards home, walking and then breaking into a run.

Tossing rocks and kicking debris along the path home, the boys are talking and skipping and running. They are lost in conversation and play when they catch sight of a pack of boys wielding rubber guns. The wild boys crouch on all fours around the edges of the houses, heads darting out long enough to sniff out the enemy and take aim.

Rubber guns—fashioned of long ribbons of innocuous looking inner-tubing stretched over lathing that has been nailed together. For tension, simple clothespins and rubber bands, and for ammunition, tailor's straight pins that draw blood when fired.

The rowdy boys, the guns, and all the while, the white wizard of progress, the most lethal enemy of all to Clayton on this day—all of these are in motion. Progress has dug a twenty-foot deep septic-tank pit in order to carry convenience to the Johnsons and other families in the vicinity. Something intended to be spectacular is coming to the neighborhood—indoor plumbing—but on this day it will wreak havoc.

Scattered, as if they had fallen randomly out of the sky and grown roots where they landed, are a handful of houses on what passes on the prairie for a city block. A couple of the houses have been built by his father's own hands, his father turning to other trades when the army sent him packing. And amidst the houses, the workers have excavated the twenty-foot pit, and outfitted it with enough stairs along the side to climb in and out.

The boys, the guns, the dark hollow pit—perhaps even this combination might not have conspired to create the ideal setting for catastrophe had it not been for the element of surprise, for the complete unpreparedness of our young boy, who makes his way home from the local country store, carrying a few ordinary items.

Yes, if not for the element of surprise, and the final wild card—dusk. That hour of the day when the world is a kaleidoscope, taking shapes and colors, real and unreal, and spinning them together until the eye is dazzled, and a little bit blind.

"Clayton! Watch out! They have rubber guns!" The other boy sees the rough kids, remembers days past, remembers their hot breath at his back, the threat of their guns pointed in his direction, yells his warning as he is running away.

Through the hazy dusk of early evening, our hero's vision is blurred by the alarm he hears in the other boy's shouts. Fear takes Clayton by the collar and spins him on his heels, yanking him this way and that. Unable to focus, unsure whether to run left or right, completely unable to gauge the distance of the armed boys, he loses his balance, and backs up.

And then it happens—that singular moment that forever changes Clayton's life. Time is suspended like an invisible trampoline that bounces him between two worlds, as he falls from this time of his life into the next, from level ground into the twenty foot septic tank pit.

~ Discernment ~

That was a pivotal moment for me, and it taught me an important lesson I'll never forget. That boy was being driven by fear, and letting myself go along with his fantasy was my undoing. After that, I never let myself get caught up in someone else's fantasy, or if I did, I did so deliberately, suspending disbelief for a good purpose, but always aware of the choices I was making.

It wasn't the danger, but his perception of the danger that was the real problem. After that, I developed the ability to think on my feet, to quickly react to my circumstances and surroundings, to never take anyone else's word for it, to measure everything for myself.

As Clayton matures, he comes to insist upon thinking for himself, and standing out rather than fitting in. But, as all children do, he starts out his life doing his best to fit in.

They'd put you in a rubber room if you stood out. You ran the risk of psychiatric intervention. "You told us right there that you believe in blank…right there! And now, we want you to speak to the company psychiatrist." And, after you they would come.

If you do what's right, don't make waves, and belong to the right associations, you can get to the top—but, at the top of every company is a big crook! He didn't start out that way, but he slowly becomes crooked. He thinks, after all, "I don't want to blow the whistle. I just want to fit in." Everyone just tries to fit in. As a result, you need a bloodbath to get rid of crooks who find their way to the top by lying, cheating, stealing.

Fitting in or standing out? Fitting in is our game. When people stand out, they're dangerous. "He will never shut up! He always has to have the last word!"

Now, on stage, they don't want you to flop—they want you to stand out. But, I know I'm going to have to pay for everything I say. Still, I tell the truth. I just try to be skillful about it. I push myself into thinking more quickly, trusting my instincts, my gift of gab, and the occasional joke.

We all have two natures in us. You've got the one that wants to discriminate and the other that wants to generalize. One is tenderhearted and one is tough-minded. They both want to live. Somehow they're in touch with each other. I learned to let my right brain rule. I like to remain in that right-brain mode of having the right to change my mind, which is how I define freedom.

Fitting in or standing out. To some extent, the creative one will stand out, be the butt of the joke, the class clown. The other one has its feelings under control, and doesn't know how it feels until it analyzes it.

These two brains are working back and forth. When you're fitting in, you're dealing with the common, ordinary marketplace. You're told by the news what to think. You won't challenge anything. You keep religion deep inside, don't get into a fight about it, don't tell people how you're going to vote because they're planning to vote for the other guy. If they're common enough, they'll develop a lifelong hatred towards you for it. "I could put up with your crap until I realized you were a Republican!"

~ Imprisonment ~

Onto a stiff bed of two by fours, garbage and litter, lands young Clayton. He has fallen into the hole. His thighbone shatters in two places upon impact, the center chunk of his thigh now pushed out of alignment with the other two sections of his leg. Lying there broken, he slips down, down into the cold vacuum of unconsciousness.

I don't know how long I lay there unconscious. When I woke up, I didn't feel woozy, and strangely, I didn't really feel any pain. I tried to sit, but couldn't get up. I just knew I was scared and weak.

From the vast cavernous hole where he lies, it seems a long way up to the face of the neighborhood boy now peeking over the edge of the pit. Clayton cries weakly, "My mom! Hurry, go get my mom!"

Soon, more faces appear along the rim of the pit, as a crowd gathers to gawk at our hero. Before long, Clayton's father makes his way down the steps cut into the side of the ditch, gathers his injured son in his arms, and like a fireman, lays him over his shoulder and carries him to safety.

It was wonderful having him save me, but it wasn't the first time. He'd saved me from nightmares before. It felt so good to know my folks were there and my father had me now, and I was safe...

They make their way above ground, and our boy sees his mother waiting at their car, and longs to feel her comforting hand stroking his hair.

"Get in the car, Mae! Please! You've got to drive us to the hospital!" His father is anxious to get his son to safety, but Mae is dazed, paralyzed into immobility by the sight of her son, broken and unable to walk. She can't seem to shove the car key into the ignition, can't take her eyes off Clayton's little face.

"All you all right, Darling?" She asks, concerned only for her son.

"Mae, please! Get with it for God's sake!" And in that moment, like the rubber band on the rubber guns, the man's patience snaps, and he feels his hand fly up to backhand his wife. "Come on! Start the damned car!"

And that does it. The nighttime comes back into sharp focus as the sting of his slap hits her face, and she sobers, starting the car.

Lying in his father's lap, watching his mother's face, feeling the car cut a swath through the blackening night, Clayton can't see beyond the stretch of evening to understand that right here, right now, his life is forever altered, changing shape and changing course.

This boy, the boy that he has been up until now, might never have become a Fictioneer. Living as he did, up until this very moment in time, completely absorbed in the outside world, he might never have stumbled upon the hidden door and sprung the trap, hurtling him into the interior world of his mind, where stories hatch.

Pulling the car up at the entrance of the grand edifice, Mae watches her husband carry little Clayton out of the car and up the magnificent stone steps into the hospital. Descending upon the young boy, the nurses lay him down upon a gurney and then fuss and tug and pull at him, until they've snipped all the clothing from his body.

Like a shimmering mirage on the hottest summer day starts to shake and recede and lose form in the shade, so the image of his parents gets more distant as they leave their child to the nurses and slowly disappear out of the hospital.

There I was, lying naked in front of all these women and I couldn't understand where my mom and dad were going. But in their hearts, they had delivered me safely into the hands of these healers and they were backing off to let them do their job and take care of me. I think my mother and father were a little bit intimidated by the doctors and nurses.

And then, like the pair of scissors cutting his clothing off his body, to leave him naked and new, Destiny snips his life of yesterday permanently off, leaving it like cuttings of film on the floor.

As the night of this endless, severed day grows weary and runs into the morning, George Clayton Johnson surrenders to the ether. Escorting him into the strange and alien existence that is to become his new life is a powerful and seductive agent… chloroform.

His saving grace will be his imagination—that and his ability to look forward to tomorrow.

My ability to look forward will stay with me throughout my life. Even when I got much older, it would always be tomorrow—not today—that was the real pull. What will be, not what is, keeps me engaged. I have lots of dreams, hopes, and prayers. What is to come always seems more real than what's actually going on.

It is 1936 and, three years into his reign, Adolf Hitler is hardening his cement grip on his disciples, and spending his days and nights weaving tighter and tighter the noose he will eventually throw around the necks of Jews everywhere.

Here at home, FM radio broadcasting is in its infancy, and with its new voice is shouting out the news that Philo Farnsworth's new invention, the television, also has a great set of lungs and spends all day long chattering away.

And in Wyoming, at Corlette Elementary School, Abie Pollock, a little Jewish boy, takes his seat in the second grade, a yarmulke on his head. He is about to become like a brother to a boy named Clayton, who will brighten his world, and one day become famous for the many stories he writes with a ball point pen, invented by Ladislo Biro the previous year.

In a hospital, where he lies with a shattered bone in his leg, George Clayton Johnson is living in another dimension. Trying to recount the horrible events in his mind, he remembers one minute walking home from the store with a boy he barely knew, and then everything leading up to his short flight into the dark pit where Hell began for him.

One day, he was happy on the prairie, and now, this room. Along each wall of what feels like an army barracks, standing at attention opposite each other, are beds. Like soldiers facing down, they line up in rows of five. Only something is off. It is as if the beds are floating in mid-air—raised so the nurses won't strain their backs by bending at the waist. They are too high to climb into, or out of—unless you don't mind breaking your neck. The awareness that liberty is just beyond his reach will instill in him a lifelong determination to preserve his liberty at all costs.

He is effectively trapped. This supposedly benign imprisonment makes a permanent imprint on Clayton's psyche and becomes one of the defining moments of his life.

~ Disillusionment ~

I am reminded of one seemingly small event that really changed me forever. It happened later in my life, when I was hanging out in pool halls, and becoming very close with my cousins, Jack and Bob. I ended up living in their house many times as a refugee, so I knew them well, and felt comfortable in their homes. Over many years, as their homes began to feel like my home, I came to believe in my cousins and me on the same side. I depended upon them to be interested in me because we were all family.

In those days, I managed to get myself pretty shaggy. I often couldn't get a haircut because I had no money. I had an arrangement at the barber shop where I would shine shoes in exchange for money to go to the movies. They liked to joke, "George needs to have his ears lowered!" That was the standard joke—"George is looking shaggy…hairy…like a girl!"

One day, there were three or four of us in the car, including my cousin, Jack, and some older boys I wanted to impress. Everyone started joking around and the next thing I knew, they were saying, "George needs a haircut!" They got me down and made a few chops at my hair before I became hysterical and got away.

They'd made a mess of my hair and damn near hurt me with the scissors. Now, I had no choice but to get a real haircut to fix the chopping they'd done. But, the true insult was being held down against my will—trapped!

Up until then, Jack was one of the most charming men in my life, and I wanted to be around him. But, after that, he was the guy who had helped them cut my hair. Jack's story was that he was trying to help. He may have been afraid the older boys were going to turn on him, but

I don't believe it, because he had a go-to-hell attitude, and was never chicken in that way.

My long hair became so important that people attacked me over it—which just made me more determined to keep it. My feeling was, to hell with you! I have already lost one of my best friends over my hair—my cousin Jack.

Later on, when my mother became ill and I went back to Wyoming to see her, I got a chance to see my cousin. His mother brought up that incident at some point, and I told Jack, "That was a sad situation because I really liked you, but it was quite apparent that things had changed." I was completely disillusioned with Jack.

That's an example of how little events can really change you permanently. There I found myself no longer being one of the boys for no damned reason I could think of other than the fact that somebody thought I needed a haircut.

~ Monsters ~

Clayton will turn seven years old lying flat on his back. A few days before his birthday, NBC television will take its first stab at programming—a thirty-minute variety show. If only he could see far enough into the future to know the part he will play in the history of television, Clayton's spirits might be greatly lifted. But, like every life on this side of the TV screen, his will unfold only one scene at a time.

There are windows, and the light breezes sneak in underneath, but the outside world is too remote and unreachable to be any consolation. Those new elements, those unquantifiable strangers that are about to irrevocably alter the landscape—Hitler, FM radio, television—do not gain entrance into this insular world of sterile shiny objects and beds as tall as men, and so for Clayton, they do not yet exist.

As the months go by, there never seems to be more than one or two others in the hospital at any one time, and so he lies alone, his inclined head skewing his vision, and he has only the tilting floor, the slanting ceiling and the endless parade of medical nightmares he faces on this frontier.

Everyone at the hospital was very sweet to me, and I remember the nurse bringing me a glass of grape juice because I was so parched from the ether. To this day, grape juice is still a special treat to me. But, even though I knew these people were helping me, they were my captors. I was just a child, terrified, and I really wanted my mama.

From time to time, my mom and dad would come and visit, and I remember one time, my aunts came, too. Everyone was very loving in the little time we spent together, but then they'd leave again, and I'd be back in the same situation. It became the only life I knew and my parents seemed so far away.

Dwarfed in his big bed, stranded without his mom and dad, far from his brothers and sister, Clayton meets loneliness for the first time. An unwanted roommate, loneliness moves right into the bed with him, refusing to leave. It is there with him as he drifts off, longing for home, and it greets him in the morning when he wakes after a fitful night of trying to sleep.

The nurses are there but, for all their apparent sovereignty, they seem to have no power over the loneliness, positioned as they seem to be, so far out of reach from the boy. He is essentially in exile.

Sequestered away and virtually unaware of the world outside the strange white room where he is being held prisoner, Clayton is about to become intimately familiar with a green monster. It comes at him from inside the gauzy cloth the doctors and nurses are forcing over his mouth and nose. That beast—chloroform—is a smothering companion, and every so often, it terrifies our boy, crawling up the side of his bed and wrapping itself around his head, choking out everything and stuffing his mind with fuzzy cotton ghosts.

"That's right, Clayton," he hears them whisper, "just breathe. Breathe! Now count backwards…ten, nine, eight…"

So there I was, this innocent little boy who broke his leg because he panicked over a friend's fantasy. And I found myself separated from my parents, in this hospital room, where it seemed to me they were trying to kill me with chloroform. They kept trying to get me to breathe in the ether, but I fought it with everything I had. I didn't want to inhale, so I'd pretend to be counting while holding my breath, but there was no way out. Before long, their voices would begin to distort, getting farther and farther away, as I fell into an interior space of exploding lights.

With chloroform, the more you get into it, the less you have of yourself, and in that mind space, I never saw pictures like you do in a dream. It was more like hurtling through space with images of concentric circles. I was diving into the center of a black hole where everything gets tighter and tighter.

Years later, when I found out about intergalactic space, I didn't find it hard to believe. Writing for Star Trek was natural for me—a perfect fit—because chloroform had been such an extraordinary experience.

They put him under the x-ray machine, and come up with a blueprint for his new life. Then they stick the long steel needle through the upper part of his leg just above the knee. They run cables along a grid above his hospital bed and hang weights from his legs, pulling and stretching the muscles.

They would come in periodically and remove the weights, and each time, it was agony. Whenever I would see them coming and realize it was that time again, I would plead with them, begging them not to do it. I tried to listen and do what they told me, but I hated all of it—the pain of removing the weights, the odor of the chloroform, the endless hours and weeks and months of waking up in a hospital bed.

This is now his life: the sickening chloroform cloth, gagging him into semi-consciousness; and, then, snap, as they break and reset the leg. Day by day, a little more weight stacked up in metal plates, some more stretching, and more false peace as the doctors let the bone start to heal on its own. Then the violence begins all over again with that nauseating sequence of ether, weights, snapping, and more stretching.

The most horrifying part of this disturbing symphony is the ultimate crescendo—the removal of the weights. After weeks and months of stretching the muscles and strengthening the bones beneath the burden of the metal weighted plates, at last the doctors lift the plates, one by one. The muscles, having been stretched beyond capacity, now begin after so long, to contract again, pressing together two bones still slightly soft.

It's strange to think that I can't even remember what dear Dr. Phelps looked like, considering he was the one who put my leg back together and couldn't have gotten paid anything because we were too poor.

So mid-1930s America metamorphoses outside the window and begins its long, dreadful march towards as yet unimagined horrors and holocaust—World War II. And at the same time, Clayton's tiny personal universe tips and turns, and keeps him tilted on his head with his lips blistered and burned.

Little does he know that his isolation is about to bring about a complete shift in the way he views the world. The utter lack of options, the vacuum of aloneness, and the verities of an intolerable hospital life all align themselves in such a way that he is primed to be seduced by the small book he is now holding in his hands.

Until his fall into the hole, our boy took the world as it presented itself to him. The tickling of his ear by the sound of a bird, the tingling of his cheeks from the snap in the cold prairie air, the thrill of outsmarting gophers—his short life had been filled with experiences and tactile sensations.

And now, for the first time since his birth, he is about to find a corridor inside his mind, the door to his imagination. He is about to discover that he can move from one dimension to the next, climb at will from one universe to another—not by force like when he is dragged down and away from reality by the heavy anchor of chloroform, but rather by choice, simply by opening the pages of a book.

Big Little Books—square books that are an inch-and-a-half fat, with a page of writing on one side and a picture on the other. They contain stories of families much like his, making the long journey west. They are adventure stories where the hero, solitary and noble, is confronted by some dark evil and prevails. These are stories like Clayton and the chloroform monster, like Clayton and the alien nurses who have him hanging upside down as they send him into excruciating pain every time they remove another steel plate.

Tarzan. Popeye. Bronc Peeler, a western story about a guy who breaks horses instead of resetting and breaking shattered legs. Dick Tracy and the villain with a gun that shoots ice pellets, so when the victim is found dead, the bullet, now melted, is undetectable.

How did they do that? How could someone kill a man and leave no trace? How could a young boy have his entire life altered in the single trip of a foot and the breaking of a leg? How could someone fall down a hole and wake to find themselves in another world entirely that bears no resemblance at all to the world as he knows it, save for the occasional visit of his parents who come and go. As the detectives in the book are scratching their heads, our young hero has a head full of questions of his own.

Short, fat little books beneath Clayton's reading level, but impossible to refuse as the only friends available day or night to help stave off the vast nothingness of lying in a hospital bed, month after month. Books he reads over and over again, like a rehearsed routine replayed between old friends.

Those books helped me to become a real good reader because I had nothing else to read. At the time, I was capable of reading pulp magazines, and I would tell my mother over and over again the kind I wanted, but no matter how well I described them, she would end up bringing me true crime magazines. I had no interest in them at all.

She kept confusing what I was trying to explain and it was very disappointing, but having nothing else but those Big Little Books made me into a real good reader. There was nothing else to do, no one to talk to at all, and I could read one of those in fifteen minutes. So that's what I did—I just read them over and over and over.

~ Adjustment ~

When the green light is finally given, Clayton at last sheds the shackles of the hospital bed where he has lived for months, and is released back into the freedom of childhood. The boy that was carried into the hospital, innocent and untried, hobbles out now on crutches, mended but very much changed.

He has been entirely absent from the second grade.

The interior world he has lived in for the past many months is now forever imprinted on his soul, and having explored the new terrain, he will not forget it. So while he returns to the little house on the prairie, happy to be home, delighted to be able to move swiftly around on crutches, chasing his siblings and friends, he is not the same boy that walked unsuspecting to the market on that fateful day.

On the face of it, life resumes its rhythms. Mae's sisters and their husbands come to welcome Clayton home, he demonstrates his prowess on crutches for his cousins, and everyone sits around with homemade ice cream cones in their hands. Life, at last, seems right side up.

What Clayton does not know is what transpired on the army base in Fort Warren, Wyoming during the many months of his stay in the hospital: As nylon stockings were, for the first time, seen shimmering on the calves of women in officer's clubs across America, an army cook named Duncan noticed one set of legs in particular. Repeatedly, he coaxed Charles Johnson's wife out onto the dance floor and away from her husband who sat watching.

Ira Spurgeon Duncan spent many nights with his arms around our boy's mother, dancing too close. The music stopped and she returned to the chair where she sat with her husband, sisters, and brothers-in-law. But her heart stayed with the cook, and never did return to Clayton's father.

Shortly after her middle son returns home, the dark beauty with the lantern eyes, who has been for so many months separated from her little Clayton, now becomes estranged from her husband.

So Clayton's father recedes from their home, man becoming apparition as he backs away slowly, step by step, until he is barely visible at all. And in Clayton's father's place, immediately steps Ira Spurgeon Duncan.

My mother was very popular and she always danced with the other soldiers, so maybe my dad didn't realize that Duncan was a threat until it was too late. And it just wasn't in his nature to fight to keep her. I'll never forget him saying, "I would never live with a woman who didn't want me." He couldn't have stayed. It would've been too humiliating for him.

When my dad left, I had no idea where he'd gone. As far as I could tell, he just disappeared. Later on, when we would see him and ask where he had been, he told us he had been all over the country, building barracks. I know he worked in Hawaii for a while.

I had a strong emotional bond with my real dad, but from my very earliest days, my deepest connection was with my mother. I was a mama's boy, so when my dad went out of my universe, I still had my universe.

One thing about my real dad for which I always had enormous admiration was the fact that even after my mother left him, he never had a bad thing to say about her. He was noble in many ways, and loving. Even as a grown man, when I would go visit him, I always knew his door was open to me.

George Clayton Johnson arrives at Corlette Elementary School and, having entirely missed the second grade, is placed in third grade. On the one hand, he is well beyond his peers—having fallen into the trenches and undergone the trauma of battles no child could possibly understand. His body bears the wounds and scars of a veteran. His mind, now whittled and honed to a sharp point by his months of self-reliance in the hospital, runs along new gullies and neural rivers, grooved by the endless months of lying in bondage in the hospital.

On the other hand, he is far *behind* his peers, having been nowhere near a school in over a year. One of his primary stumbling blocks is the fact that he has missed the multiplication and division lessons taught in second grade.

Approaching the front of the school on this day, he is spun around by the whirr of a boy zooming by on a bicycle. He watches the bike skidding to a sharp stop at the bike rack. Standing mute, watching this incredibly swift machine, Clayton is joined by another boy—Abie Pollock. He is equally dumbfounded.

There I am in school for the first time in a long time, and now I'm at a serious disadvantage. I'm behind in my studies, I've spent months in the hospital and my leg is messed up, and I need to know—what are the rules? What is the best group to be a part of? Who should I avoid?

I inherently understood about the sacredness of personality. It was one of the things that had drawn me to Charlie Peterson. He glittered with unique qualities.

Another one of my closest friends when I was growing up was David Sprinkle, and I spent a lot of time over at his house. I knew what was expected of me, and I was treated like family. They were very religious Christians and I knew how to survive in that environment. Eating dinner at their house was a big ceremonial thing where everyone around the table was supposed to quote a verse from the Bible. So David taught me the phrase, 'Jesus wept.' It was perfect. It was short enough to remember and yet it constituted a complete sentence.

With David, I felt a wonderful sense of freedom because I trusted and respected him, and yet I didn't have to do what he said.

I'd had friends like Charlie and David that I'd known all my life, but now for the first time, I was experiencing what people that don't know you put you through in order to size you up. I was always fascinated by the question of how people get together. So much of it is psychological.

When I met Abie, all these things were running through my mind about where I fit in with the kids at school. All my life, I had grown up with the words from the Bible, and I had heard about Jews, and now I was actually meeting one. Christians seemed to consider Jews of a lower order, but I didn't understand that.

I liked Abie right away. He had a birthmark in the form of a large mole on his upper cheek. It was a patch of brown fur, like a mouse's back. After a while, I grew accustomed to it and it wasn't a big deal, but I had never seen anything like it. I could tell that Abie was no threat to me. It was one of the main reasons we became friends. I knew he'd never hurt me.

Clayton is eight years old when he—this small, fair, towheaded boy with a bad leg—forms an alliance of the heart with a sweet little Jewish boy whose father works in a tailor's shop. Together, they sit, day in and day out. They are involved in the monotonous drone of learning the Palmer Method of Penmanship in school. Side by side, they practice forming perfect loops in cursive, and precise up and down printing strokes.

Returning home from school one day, Clayton is met at the door by the sound of Cole Porter crooning from the radio, and swirls of jasmine incense tickling his nose. Inside his house, adorned in a perfectly blocked hat, black corduroy trousers, and luminously shined black shoes, is his new stepfather. He is sitting on the edge of a chair, clean-shaven, his arms draped around the boy's mother.

Mae's head is thrown back in laughter. Her body is swaying to the music. Three or four other couples raise their beer glasses, nod, and carry on their conversation.

"Oh Darling, come in! Let me introduce you!"

Mae leads little Clayton in and shows him off to everyone. Then, as if he is twenty-eight years old instead of only eight, he becomes one more guest at the party.

This was one of my first impressions of Ira Spurgeon Duncan—coming home to find this party. It was so strange to see this man coming out of the bedroom, slapping his knee at some joke. I remember being allowed to be sort of in on it, even though I was a kid and I wasn't drinking.

The smoke, the incense, listening to that romantic music—it all made me think of foreign places. The conviviality, my mother holding court with all these people I didn't know...my home life was definitely changing.

The utter totality of his mother's love for him, the abiding confidence he had that Mae would always love him and answer any questions he might pose—these elements of their relationship saved Clayton from seeing his mother's new love as a threat to him.

Accepting my stepfather was just part of my job of comprehending my mom, part of being loyal to her in spite of the fact that I might not have understood what she was doing. If anyone had become aggressive or threatening with her, I'd have definitely gotten distressed, but as long as she was happy, I was happy.

I never got the sense that Duncan replaced me in her affections, and I knew I had the inside track. Whatever I needed to know, she'd explain it to me like a grown-up. Somehow, I was in on the secret.

At the end of her life, we were talking about what happens after death, and I said to her, "Mom, it wouldn't be Heaven for me unless you were in it," and she said, "You're in my Heaven, too." That was a moment of great candor, of really laying ourselves bare to each other, but I always had that feeling with her—that she loved me and took me seriously.

It is now 1937, the year Adolf Hitler supporters gather to hear his intentions to acquire "living space" for the German people; and the year Japanese forces invade China in the battle of Lugou Bridge. In London, the BBC beats America to the punch with the first high-definition television broadcasts. Here at home, the technology is introduced that makes it possible to generate high-powered UHF-TV; CBS Television begins TV development; and the first issue of *Look* goes on sale.

Years later, I would be standing on a street corner as a young man, to get a look at one of my first TV screens. I was in downtown L.A., gazing into the window of Broadway Department Store, where they had plugged in a TV set and allowed passersby to watch through the window. You could see Uncle Miltie [Milton Berle], Liberace, and a wrestling match, as they piped the sound into the street.

~ Imagination ~

This same year, Mae Johnson Duncan, her children, and her new husband rent an apartment behind the tailor shop where Joseph Pollock—Abie's Dad—lives with his family. It is not long before she is pregnant. Soon, Clayton has a half-brother and half-sister, fraternal twins. Ira Spurgeon Duncan and his new wife are in Heaven with baby Kenneth and baby Kathleen.

Sitting cross-legged and hunched over on a wooden bench in his shop is Abie's father. He rarely speaks to his children. When he does speak, it's in a language that young Clayton cannot understand. Years later, our young hero will wonder whether it was Polish, Yiddish, Hebrew, or German his friend's dad was speaking. What he knows for certain is that his new friend, Abie, and his foreign father, do not share the same kind of kinship that Clayton shares with Mae.

His school studies skip cavalierly ahead of Clayton, and he strives vainly to keep up, but he falls further and further behind. He begins to feel incrementally more and more alienated. He is walking, quite literally, out of step with his peers.

It was at this point in my life that I began to feel myself at a serious disadvantage, and that feeling began to determine the course of my life. I found myself in a position where I was always trying to find ways to overcome that and be looked up to, respected and acknowledged as a peer—or even someone extraordinary.

There was one important thing I learned in this early period of being behind in school: every room you walk into has instructions built into it, if you know how to interpret them. Where the desk is placed, where the teacher stands, where the clock is, where the students are expected to sit—all of this is arranged to be instructive and let you know your place in the room. And later in life, I realized that where the executive sits, where his desk is placed in his office at the production studio—all of it is arranged and designed to be instructive, as well.

Once I'd grown up, sometimes for amusement and story research, I would arrange meetings with people, knowing full well there was no work to be had. And when I arrived, I would intentionally go against the status quo, behaving contrary to what was expected of me. If they expected me to walk in and sit down opposite the desk, I might go and stand behind the person's desk. Or stand underneath the clock. If someone offered me coffee, I might say no, but do you have any grape juice? In this way, I maintained some kind of an advantage over the situation.

It's funny, but if people think they're dealing with someone just like them, they immediately lose respect for you. If they see you as an enigmatic character beyond their comprehension—well, then, that they can trust. In their perception, that's what an artist should be.

I also learned later in life that if you meet with people you've never met before, whether they are old or young, and your reputation precedes you, you have the advantage. The known one in the room is automatically deferred to as the teacher. It is human nature. Everything is ultimately psychological.

The merry-go-round of third-grade life spins all the other children around and around. Clayton watches them pass him by, laughing and screaming, but finds it increasingly more and more difficult to jump aboard.

Although he has lost his academic edge during his time recuperating, he has become a natural student of human nature. And he is prodigious. His mental instrument is becoming more and more acute. He calculates and assesses, intuits and strategizes, forecasts and projects what any given character might do in any particular situation, given an ever changing set of variables.

He is discovering what he needs to know about himself and others so that the tornado which has rearranged his life might not prove to have dealt him a fatal blow. He is using these exercises to save his life—or at least, preserve a place for himself. But what he perceives as a shield against the cruelty of fate will actually prove to be much more than his greatest weapon against the ill tides.

The instinctive character study in which he is engaged is going to serve him well. Over the months and years ahead, his penchant for all things related to human nature will begin to paint for him a life infinitely more textured, colorful, and fulfilling than the bleak and frightening future he fears his disadvantages might subject him to.

One year after AT&T lays the first experimental coaxial cable lines connecting New York and Philadelphia, little George Clayton Johnson inadvertently enrolls himself in his own personal communications course. Side by side with Abie Pollock, his brother in soul, Clayton retreats to the landscape of imagination. He is naturally gravitating towards the one world he instinctively understands—the movies. In the cool expanse of the movie theaters, our hero spends every hour he can studying the art of telling stories for the screen.

In those years Clayton spends with his friend Abie and all their on-screen heroes—some of whom he will meet later in life!—George Clayton Johnson enters his cocoon and begins to metamorphose. Day by day, he grows into the one thing he was always destined to be: a Fictioneer.

~ Cinema ~

In November of 1938, Nazi paramilitary troops and civilian sympathizers manage to bring so much destruction to the Jews in a single night that the event is dubbed Kristallnacht—the Night of Broken Glass. Thousands upon thousands of Jewish businesses are looted and burned, hundreds of synagogues set on fire, almost one hundred Jews murdered, and at least 25,000 Jewish men put under arrest.

That same year will see the building of the Neuengamme and Mauthausen concentration camps. While the world sinks into this insanity, our little blond boy and his Jewish pal will spend many days seated shoulder to shoulder at the movies.

Also this year, Orson Welles' radio broadcast, *War of the Worlds*, will cause mass hysteria and confusion in the eastern United States, proving that the net cast over the collective psyche of the American people by a compelling story can be hypnotic, indeed.

Meanwhile, Mae's new marriage has its foundation deep in the heart, and everyone believes it cannot be shaken. But, she and her brood must learn to live with an absentee husband, as Ira Spurgeon Duncan is often called off the army base and sent away on assignment. Nevertheless, the presence of the new babies—now bringing the number of Johnson/Duncan kids up to six—is a source of unbounded joy. Everyone is in love with the babies, and this love spills over onto each other as well, tying together and unifying this blended family.

Clayton loves his newest little siblings, and he has found another new love, as well, every bit as powerful and enduring…

Abie and I loved the movies. There were three theaters that all stood on this alley in downtown Cheyenne. We'd take the quickest route from one movie to the next, down the alley, where we'd find these cardboard boxes.

As the machinery of industry continues to churn, retail stores fill their racks and windows. In come the cardboard boxes, filled with finery. Out comes the finery onto the displays, out into the alleys go the boxes, and here comes our fearless twosome ready to pounce on an opportunity. Clayton and Abie quickly rummage through the boxes to find the best of the lot—the right sizes, tops still on, in good condition—and off they go to make any deal that will fill their pockets with coins.

We'd take ten or twelve boxes and sell them to the Wigwam Bakery for twenty or thirty cents. Then, we could use that money to go to the movies. One of our greatest discoveries was when we figured out that the usher at one of the theaters loved Cherry Cokes. From then on, we knew that instead of paying ten cents each to get into the movies, we could take one dime, bribe the usher with a Cherry Coke and both get in for free.

Our twosome also becomes a familiar sight at the salvage yard. Copper wire, an old battery, the remainder of a tool, any found object they might be able to turn into cash—these things they brush off, shine up, and exchange for coins at the salvage yard. Streets lined with apartments are a gold mine. All it takes is a boost up onto the fire escape and then these two can stealthily prowl around for coke bottles and milk bottles. Once they have the bottles in hand, they carefully make their way across the roofs and back down to the street.

Every day we found some new way to make money. The ice plant was one of our favorites. We got a wagon from somewhere, and we'd take it to the ice plant where these huge fifty-to-a-hundred-pound blocks of ice would come sliding out these doors. The ice plant was right beside the railroad tracks, and they would fill these refrigerated railcars with ice and keep them cold enough to ship lettuce or melons or whatever they were selling.

We discovered there was a hatch on the top of the railcars. So we would open the hatch, and down below, we could see this metal-lined pit that was full of ice. While the railcars were sitting there, we could check to see if there were any ice chips that hadn't yet melted that we could sell to the neighborhood. Then we would lower ourselves down through the hatch, scoop up some ice, and cart it off in our wagons.

Everyone had an icebox, so they would pay us ten to fifteen cents for some ice. And we'd use the money to take a bus to the lake—or the movies.

In those days, they had the serials. It was commonplace for a theater to show two killer movies, or even three or four of them at a time, and we'd sit through them twice. Going to the movies was an all-day affair. I learned to walk into the movies backwards so it seemed like I was coming out, and then I could work my way back in.

It didn't take long for us to become very familiar with the old Princess Theaters. There were wings on either side, as if it were a live theater and there were actors backstage. We loved to roam around back there. We would wait until the projectionist had started the film and left the booth, and then we would get up on the stage and walk behind the silver screen. We rarely got caught. There we were, in this huge room, and there was this huge light being cast upon the screen. If you walked behind it, you could see the light reflecting off the screen.

I was totally enamored of the movies and loved everything about them. They were always a great escape for me. I'll never forget the first movie I ever saw. It was called The Ghost Goes West. It was about a castle that was shipped from England to America, and the castle ghost stows away on the ship.

The second movie I ever saw was Frankenstein, and it will forever live in my mind. It was the scariest, most bizarre thing I'd ever seen and it was too bloody much for my mind. The themes of that movie are so universal; they are at the center of every friendship. Everyone loved Frankenstein, and he was brought back to life from death, just like the primordial energies of the universe brought me back to life after my fall.

Abie and I would spend a long time discussing the movies after we left the theater. He liked Gene Autry and Roy Rogers but they were too civilized for me. I wanted a cowboy with some hair on his chest. I remember seeing Flash Gordon conquer the universe, and there was a hero named the Green Archer who was a take-off on Robin Hood. He was a killer who dressed in a green costume and fired arrows from a bow.

After I'd seen a movie, I could always tell the entire story to someone. It would amaze people. If someone had the attention span, and was *willing to give me twenty minutes, I really could recount the movie in its entirety. And that's what gave me my status with the other kids.*

By stepping inside the film, by projecting himself up onto the screen and into the story, by inhaling and ingesting the stories he sees projected, Clayton begins to blur the line between his cinema life and his real life. At the same time, he learns to use each one to understand, affect, calculate, navigate, and interpret the other.

It is this newfound aptitude of Clayton's—to see and comprehend a movie so completely that he can re-enact it with every nuance and subtlety of character and plot—that gives him a leg up. With this toolbox of imagination and insight, found in a movie theater of all places, he is co-writing his own destiny. He is upping the odds that he may be what many others in these unfortunate times may not—a survivor.

At last, he has found a way out of the hole. His understanding of psychological motives and drives, combined with his natural taste for a story, is becoming the rope thrown over the side of the ditch by which he can hoist himself up and out. At last he has stumbled upon a way to stand not only head to head with his peers, but even apart. The chance to be outstanding, revered, admired, and respected is within his grasp. He has found a means to make a success of himself—a seeing eye dog to accompany him along the sometimes dark pathways of life.

This gift that our hero now possesses is a magical set of tools. It is a psychological system of comprehension that our boy can apply to anyone, however complex, in any situation.

On the world stage, the worst kind of aberrant behavior is afoot. Everyone everywhere is growing increasingly aware that Hitler—this ruler who has infiltrated and infected the minds of the German people like a noxious gas released into the air—is forever changing not only Germany, but the entire world.

At Clayton's home, major change is brewing as well.

"Where is she?" Ira Spurgeon Duncan demands of his stepson. "Where's Mae?"

Duncan carefully sets down his hat and looks around the apartment in disgust. Beds with their wrinkled sheets and crumpled covers mock him. Dishes crowded together in the sink, unwashed, stare at him. "Look at this place! Where is your mother?"

But the question is a rhetorical one, for both the big man and the little one know exactly where she is. She is where she always is these days. Whenever her husband, the army cook, is away on assignment, Mae Johnson Duncan is, inevitably, downtown, looking at the world through the thick golden fog of alcohol. And this day, she is not expecting him back in town.

Ira demands, "Do you know where she is or not?"

Clayton shrugs his shoulders, and simply says, "I'm hungry. I've been home alone all day and I'm really hungry."

Ira says, "She's at the bar, isn't she? Look at this place!"

"I'm really hungry," the boy repeats.

Distracted, Duncan turns on his shiny black heel, marches over to the cupboard, and pulls down a can of green beans. And then the man whose job it is to cook food worthy of our American soldiers, sticks a fork in the cold beans and hands it to his stepson. "Here. Eat this." Then he turns and leaves to go find his wife.

My stepfather never wanted to assume any lordly prerogatives over me. I've never had a collar. In the life of most boys, there comes a point in time where the father either backs away or confronts the kid, and usually if they back away, the kid becomes a thug. But my real father was gone, and Duncan never attempted to have dominion over me. I think he was as leery of me as I was of him.

My mama was everything to me. I wondered if that was how Jesus felt: "Sure, Joseph was running around, but I was a mama's boy and my world was all about Mary."

Whatever my mother told me to do, I did it. I was tremendously obedient. She didn't have to try to discipline me, because whatever she wanted, I was happy to do it. Maybe that's why my stepfather never tried to bend my will to his. In my entire life, I've never made that submission to anyone.

~ Change ~

In 1939, Adolf Hitler's troops trample and overrun Poland, starting World War II. In contrast, that very same year, Frank Sinatra gives his premier performance at the Paramount Theatre in New York.

Also that year, in New York City, RCA and Vladimir Zworykin conduct experimental broadcasts from the Empire State Building. And, amid the drums of battle sounding in the distance, and the increasingly ominous gathering of momentum turning the wheels of War, there is the World's Fair, where television is demonstrated.

An early World's Fair prospectus states, "The Fair will dramatically display the most promising developments of ideas, products, services, and social factors of the present day in such a fashion that the visitor may gain a vision of what he might attain for himself and for his community by intelligence and cooperative planning."

The RCA exhibit at the Fair is used as a showcase for the first televised speech by a president, Franklin Delano Roosevelt, who addresses the opening day crowds. Also on display are RCA's new line of television receivers, some of which have to be coupled with a radio if you want to hear sound. It is a big year for broadcast communications: the Dumont Company starts making television sets.

That year, as well, John Atanasoff is building the first computer, Chester Carlson is running to the patent office with the plans for his Xerox copier, and Germans are flying the first jet-powered airplane. So the Brits are devising microwave technology to detect enemy planes.

Albert Einstein proposes the atomic bomb. And a team of scientists led by President Roosevelt's science adviser commandeer five labs at Bell Labs, Cal-Tech, Harvard, MIT and the Carnegie Institution to help persuade the president to go through with building the bomb.

It is almost as if the earth itself, shifting with the rumblings of volcanic political and social change, is, by some majestic act of nature, exploding in a lava flow of new inventions, one of the most significant of which is the television. For there are things happening around the world that simply must be told. And more than that, they must be seen to be believed.

So this invention which is barely a handful of years old matures instantaneously. Like an eight-year-old boy forced to become a man when his father leaves home. Like a young wife, forced into maturity when she watches her uniformed husband waving goodbye from the window of a train.

From the rural train station platforms to the World's Fair in New York City, everyone feels America metamorphose into something as yet unforeseen.

Writing in the New York Times, H. G. Wells says, in this astounding display of prescience:

"The visitor who wants to get the most out of this World's Fair will do best to regard it not as a show of things, but let his imagination off the leash of discretion for a bit. Then he may really get a glimpse of the realities of tomorrow that lurk in this jungle of exhibits. It will cease to look like a collection of things for sale and reveal its real nature as a gathering of live objects, each of which is going to do something to him, possibly something quite startling, before he is very much older. The World of Tomorrow," continued Wells, "is arranged not as the visible rendering of a utopian dream but to assemble before us what can be done with human life today, and what we shall almost certainly be able to do with it, if we think fit, in the near future."

"A glimpse of the realities of tomorrow … each of which is going to do something to him, possibly something quite startling, before he is very much older." Although H.G. Wells writes this and it is printed in a noted newspaper thousands of miles away in a city where George Clayton Johnson has never set foot, he could be describing the path that life will unfold for our hero.

In our hero's home, little Kenneth and Kathleen are learning to toddle around the Duncan apartment, and Abie Pollock and Clayton are walking tall like real men, prowling the back alleys looking for enterprising ways to make a buck.

Meanwhile, Cheyenne celebrates its pioneer spirit with a huge Fourth of July carnival. It is not a big city and it is not the World's Fair, but this is the biggest thing these prairie families will see this year.

Cheyenne Frontier Days.

I'll never forget Frontier Days and all those cowboys. Montana, Colorado, Wyoming—that was all part of a glorious Old West, and Cheyenne celebrated it. I always felt a little weird knowing that everything I saw in all those western movies was a real part of my life.

And on that day, with the weather like mama's hand stroking your face, everyone at the parade is sure that whatever the talk of war, nothing could be as bad as all that. Covered wagons line up and men in tall hats with stiff necks and jutted chins beat big drums and follow the wagons down the main street of the town. Girls twirl batons. Others sit atop the wagons in floppy bonnets with satin ribbons, and wave the queen's wave. Their faces are cemented into ladylike grins.

Comanche and Cheyenne Indians form a circle, and dance around a fire. Clayton watches their moccasins, watches their heads bobbing up and down, notices the quickness of their legs. He looks at the feathers on the headdresses. And again he thinks of the movies.

There we were, the last stop on the Union Pacific Railroad as it expanded and built its way out west. The history of the state is all about cowboys and Indians. The very essence of my hometown... "Cheyenne, Wyoming, out where the West began," sounds like the beginning of a movie.

Execution, one of the Twilight Zone stories I will write years later, may have had its first seed in Cheyenne's Frontier Days. Execution was based on an idea that has always fascinated me—divine retribution...a guy digs his own grave...what you sow is what you reap...what goes around comes around. It's wisdom fiction. It's moral. A vast mystery becomes clear—be careful what you wish for, you may get it. If you can get into more of a thought territory in the story, you can show God's prankish hand in things.

After the parade, real live cowboys, their muscled thighs and calves wrapped in denim and leather, leap upon the ferocious spines of wild horses and bulls, and force them to the ground. Later, as the night sky pops and crackles and breaks out in hysterical colors and shouts, the smell of sulfur and smoke from the fireworks reaches the noses of Clayton and Abie, who have their heads tilted up to the sky.

"They say that Hitler is going to try to kill all the Jews," Abie says.

"But who is he?" Clayton wonders. "Is he a monster, like Frankenstein? Or a villain like the Green Archer?"

Boom! The staccato explosions sound like bombs. Beneath the neon green of the Ferris wheel overhead, people cannot help but think about the war. And with their fingers sticky with the bleeding pink of cotton candy, the boys are quiet for a minute.

When the band takes a break and the makeshift dance floor clears, Clayton gives Abie the signal and they fly underneath the bandstand, feeling in the dark for quarters and pocketing them for the movies.

Crawling out, their knees wet with mud, Clayton says, "I've been thinking about it and there's no way. It's simply impossible. I don't know who Hitler is, but even if someone went around all day and night for a month, and they shot at every Jew they saw, they still couldn't kill them all, could they?"

The boys look at each other and shrug, but somewhere deep inside, Clayton wonders. He is beginning to see far beyond the confines of his own experience, and deep into the human psyche. This will come in handy when he begins writing for *The Twilight Zone*.

Everyone carries a psychological world around with them—what they believe is true. The ultimate story is the Truth with a capital "T." Everyone has their own reality, but those realities are the truth with a small "t." Truth with a small "t" is really perception; it's not what is. Someone may perceive that all those people standing around on the street are secret agents, but no, they're not—they're shopping! That's the Truth.

Later, when I start writing for The Twilight Zone, I will come to understand that the show is psychological drama. It's about what he thinks is true and what she thinks, not what is and what isn't true. He thinks that if the clock stops, he's going to die, and she thinks he's an addled old man. Or, she thinks he's out to kill her, and he thinks she's a crazy old woman. Which one is real?

In psychological drama, it's not about what's really happening. But the reader—or the viewer—is a different spectator. As a spectator from without, they see what each character thinks is true, fits it all together, and comes to some sort of conclusion about what they believe to be the message or the theme of the story.

~ Tragedy ~

Duncan sits at the kitchen table in their small apartment behind the Pollock's. His pants are perfectly creased and he furrows his brow as he reads the newspaper.

Clayton stands back at a short distance, sees the picture of the Fuhrer addressing a crowd from a balcony, and tries to read over his stepfather's shoulder.

Duncan says, "Damn that Hitler! How could they let that sonofabitch get away with this, Mae? How could they?"

"Duncan! The babies!" Mae coos to little Kathleen and Kenneth.

"Who is this Hitler, anyway?" Clayton wants to know.

"Who's Hitler?!" Duncan shakes his head and chuckles.

Clayton asks, "What is really going on? Abie and I keep hearing things about him, but can it really be possible…?"

Duncan was cold, courteous, and perfectly happy being remote. He was above me, distant and unconcerned. After all, he didn't marry my mother for the kids, but along with her came a wagonload of us kids.

When I tried to ask, "Who's Hitler? What's this all about?" He just kept muttering invectives and I almost felt like he was deliberately teasing me. Hitler was someone I should know about, but he wasn't about to explain anything to me. It made me wary of trying to get close to him.

If I tried to tell him anything, I got the distinct feeling he had judged me and found me unworthy. On top of all that, I was always guarding what I said to him because I didn't want to be leaking my mother's secrets. Everything combined to make me feel like I didn't want to really get close to him.

That winter, on a frigid night at ten o'clock, Charlie Johnson Duncan, Clayton's big brother, clocks out, says goodnight to the front desk clerk and the doorman at the hotel where he works, and comes home. When he gets inside, the other five kids—Clayton, Ronnie, Ramona and the twins, Kenneth and Kathleen, are all fast asleep.

Rubbing his hands together, the feeling returns to his numb digits and his teeth stop chattering. So he takes off his big sheepskin coat, takes off his bellhop hat, and tiptoes over to check on the twins.

Standing over the babies as they sleep, Charlie smiles, then frowns, aware of the sharp chill in the air. He decides to carefully lay his coat over their cold, tiny feet. Then he takes off his uniform, stretches his back, stiff from carrying too many suitcases that night, and goes in to brush his teeth before falling asleep.

The following morning, Clayton and his brothers and sisters are awakened by a scream. From that netherworld where sleep is retreating and daylight has not yet reached his bedside, Clayton struggles to understand what he is hearing.

"Mama?" He fights through the fog of sleep like he used to fight off the ether.

Clayton asks, "Mama? What is it, Mama?"

Mae is standing over him now, tears springing from her face. She collapses on the side of his bed and takes him in her arms. "Oh, Clayton, Clayton... It's the babies. They are dead. Suffocated. Oh, how could he? How could he...?"

"Get dressed now, son, and run across the street," Duncan orders, as he takes Mae in his arms and tries to comfort her. His own voice is wooden and flat, like the underside of a coffin.

"Run! Hurry, son! Call the fire department!" Duncan urges him.

Clayton pulls on his pants, his mind scrambling to find the missing puzzle pieces that will make this horrific scene comprehensible. "But, I don't understand... how? What happened to them? How did it happen?" And as he flies across the street to the telephone at the grocery store, tears sting his eyes and his heart is leaden.

Neither Mae nor Ira Spurgeon Duncan can bear the sight of the cold bodies of the twins, laid toe to toe. Neither of them can look squarely at what has happened. And so the couple, each in their own way, turns to their own sorrow.

And in the palpable emptiness that now chokes out all joy in the home, Charlie, Clayton, Ramona and Ronnie are left with little. For anyone can see that their mother, stricken by this tragedy like a mighty tree beneath the sudden impossibility of a lightning bolt, is wandering farther and farther from their stepfather each day.

The remaining children sit in the hard oak pews and watch the shoeboxes holding their little siblings lowered down into the earth and smothered in dirt. They have each one become a ship, unable to bear the storm alone, but too weak to reach the great yacht, their mother, who is floundering as well under the assault of the tempest.

Their mother, the one certainty they had always counted on, has lost heart. Worse than that, she has lost her will to hold on—not to life, no, it isn't breathing that she lets go of when the twins dies, but something of her soul. And the hand of her new husband.

As for Charlie, he is shattered. His well-intentioned attempt to warm the cold feet of his beloved little brother and sister went dreadfully awry. And, he can no longer find his own reflection in the broken glass all around them. So Charlie drifts irrevocably from the rest of the family.

The babies—gone. Ira and Mae—over. Charlie—devastated and exiled by his own hand.

It is 1940, and, along with George Clayton Johnson and his family from the prairie, people everywhere are reeling from the thunderous crack of the sky falling. It is the jarring crash as the world gets crushed under the weight of history's most preventable and destructive train wreck: the Holocaust. America's first third-term president, FDR, has a full plate.

Meanwhile, Italian filmmaker Bernardo Bertolucci, Al Pacino, and future Beatles, Ringo Starr and John Lennon, are infants. Also brought into the world that same year is George Takei, who will later become well known on a television series, the premiere episode of which will be penned by George Clayton Johnson: *Star Trek*.

Not a single Nobel prize is awarded that year. World War II is in full swing.

The Johnson-Duncan family is irrevocably shattered. And George Clayton Johnson turns eleven years old.

Once the babies were born and then died, Charlie felt absolutely rotten. That was the end of him in the family. He felt himself an outcast.

He disassociated himself, and turned himself away from us. After that, he took to either working for himself, staying with my Aunt Verna at her house, or staying with other people—anything but being at home. I never felt badly towards him and was later astonished at what a great success he made of himself as a specialist in radar.

~ Alienation ~

When the glue that holds the family together is dissolved by this horrible tragedy, it is like each member of the family slips away from the dock, small boats adrift on a lake.

The babies are dead and there is no longer a household. So, young Clayton and his siblings spend years being farmed out to various relatives, and enduring several moves, as his mother comes and goes and his father is God knows where.

What little money there was went mostly to alcohol so my mother could retreat from the overwhelming situation in which we found ourselves. We had no permanent household, and it led to a series of moves. The situation really became hopeless. We had no furniture, no radio, no television, no books. The kitchen cabinets were always empty. Not only were we broke, but we were demoralized from a lack of stability.

My mother had come from a backwoods farm, and quit school when she was in the third grade to help around the house. Now, she was married, and needed leadership, but in many ways, she was still just a child, herself. Her first husband—my father—gave her leadership, but he was boring. She left him for a more interesting man, but that man was now off and gone, and she had no leadership.

She let her children raise her children. It calls to mind the Twilight Zone story, Kick the Can. That's the way it was in my world. Being raised by other children, everything I know today I learned from playing games—how to hold a fork, how to say "Yes, sir!" and "No, sir!" and how to read.

My life was an endless series of relatives and schools—fifteen or sixteen schools. There was no continuity, no depth of any kind. I was ignorant except for my reading. I found ways to get books and magazines. Maybe

I'd find them in a train station, and take them home to look at later. When it came to reading, I was indefatigable.

At last, there came a time when my mother truly lost it and was sent into rehab for the drying out process. The authorities appointed a probation officer to her case. To their eyes, here was a lady—my mother—who, for all intents and purposes was a drunk with a bunch of kids. My siblings and I were taken away from her and separated.

I ended up staying with my old friend, David Sprinkle, and his family, who were receiving some sort of stipend from the State in return for looking after me. I think the state was paying Mrs. Sprinkle thirty dollars a month to care for me. I ate and slept with her children, took her orders, and lived in her environment.

Later on, when the situation deteriorated even further, my mother signed a paper over to Mrs. Sprinkle so that she would take care of my kid brother, Ronnie, on the same terms as she'd taken care of me. My mother would literally say, "I give him up," which devastated my brother. It's a terrible situation when she actually gives you away.

My time with the Sprinkles couldn't last forever. The orphanage came to get me.

~ The Orphanage ~

I was at the Sprinkle house when the orphanage came for me. My clothes had been cleaned, and I had gathered my possessions. My little sister, Ramona, was already in the car when it pulled up. I also had two more little sisters at this point (the offspring of my mother and stepfather)— Judy and Lola Merle—and Mom kept them with her.

To David Sprinkle it was, for all intents and purposes, his very own brother they were taking from him that day. After all, the boys had been living as family. As the strange middle-aged lady ushers our young hero into her car, David's eyes well up with tears. To make matters even worse, it slowly becomes clear that Clayton is getting dropped off in Casper, Wyoming, and his dear sister, Ramona, at a different location—the Sheridan Girls' School.

I was fourteen years old when I was sentenced to the orphanage and my sister was sentenced to the girls' school. After I bid my sister goodbye, I was taken possession of and placed in a dormitory with a housemother. If I'd been sixteen years old, I would have been sent down the road to the brick building where the older boys lived. They worked on the irrigation ditches for the farm where we raised our own food.

It was a boring existence, with nothing for us boys to do. We were let outside and we'd sit around under stunted trees, or swing on a swing set. I didn't know who to talk to or where I would be welcome.

I had the strongest feeling that I'd been there before…the building, the look of the skyline…it was the strongest sense of déjà vu. To amuse myself, I'd look around, trying to anticipate what was behind a certain door, and the housemother would catch me and demand to know, "What are you doing here?"

I'd say, "Oh, just looking at these windows." I got a reputation with the housemother as an "Alibi Ike" type of guy—a character from the comic strips who always has a reason for what he's doing.

I didn't let the other kids intimidate me, and they didn't like that, so they would try to gang up on me. I was willing to take them all on, and the housemother had to be called. "Clayton," she said to me, "you are giving me a chronic bellyache!"

I soon discovered that I had influence over the children because I could tell stories. I talked about the Lone Ranger, Flash Gordon, and Ming the Merciless, played by Cy Charles Middleton, with his drooping Oriental mustaches, his long and lean bony face, his headdress, and his big cape. There would be tons of guards around, but Ming the Merciless did exactly as he pleased, and walked around saying things like, "Seize them, you fool!" He was the ruler of the planet Mongo, planning to invade earth.

From time to time, Clayton's mother comes to visit him at the orphanage. She arrives at the fence and asks one of the boys to go get Clayton. She has brought her son a gift—a pocketknife, but it is only a matter of minutes before it ends up in the hands of the housemother.

There was a shop guy who took care of the place, and with his help, one boy had made a little tank out of lathing, with nails tacked together, and a gun pointing out of a turret. When I saw it, I knew I could make things like that, but I needed a knife. Once the pocketknife from my mom made it into the desk drawer of the lady in charge, I pleaded my case, bringing along the tank the other boy had made. I explained, "I could make stuff like that but we don't have any tools!"

She opened her drawer, looked at the half dozen knives that were in there, picked up my knife, thought about it for a minute, and then put it back inside and closed the drawer. But, the next day, the shop guy came out with a couple of little saws for me to use. The first thing I made was a rubber gun.

It is a very powerful memory—these boys and girls. They were orphans and they knew it. Each of them had no hope and no education. They were illiterate, by and large. But, there was a room full of books you could go into from time to time, where they had a broken set of Dickens, a complete set of Mark Twain or Jack London—all those books people donate to the orphanage.

Without any true friends in the orphanage, Clayton seeks out adventure stories, and sits on a bench in that room, getting lost in the books for a couple of hours at a time. He doesn't feel threatened by the authority figures who bustle around, looking officious and jangling their keys, but it is a library of some kind, and sounds do echo, so he does sometimes hear, "Shh!"

The older boys take turns at various tasks, and then on Sunday mornings, after the chores are done, they all file into the dining room for all-you-can-eat cinnamon rolls and pitchers of hot cocoa. After breakfast, everyone files upstairs, wriggles into the suits they've been provided, and boards the bus to church.

There was a wire fence between the boys' and girls' sections. The boys would go towards the girls' sections on different occasions. One boy, Billy Solheim, had a sister over there, and my sister, Ramona, could have been next door for all I knew. Billy and his sister would stand by the fence, talking. The officials didn't like it, but Billy never got punished for it. I think mostly, the officials wanted to keep the girls manageable, and that was easier if there were no boys to provoke them. They didn't want the girls playing for a different audience.

Everyone told us what to do, and one person or another would guide us through this sterile environment, day in and day out. Everything was orchestrated in such a way as to keep the environment common, instead of rich, intriguing, and fascinating.

Perhaps it is here that Clayton develops his lifelong determination to preserve his liberty, and to remain, as he puts it, "a dog without a collar."

~ INDEPENDENCE ~

Under the guidance of a probation officer, Mae learns that if she can find a job, she can get her children back in her care.

She was in a hopeless situation, without food to feed her children, accepting various kinds of help. One of her sisters scraped up enough money to rent a dismal place in the deceptively named Golden West Hotel on the sandbar of the polluted Platte River in the slums of Casper, Wyoming. Then, they opened a laundry. With a couple of huge sinks and huge tables, and access to hot water, they were able to take in laundry.

The probation officer is satisfied with Mae's new employment, and allows her to go pick up Clayton from the orphanage. He is finally reunited with Ramona and free from the orphanage!

Only, now, Clayton finds he cannot make himself succumb to the authority figures at school, and often ditches classes. The police find him, clean him up, and deliver him back to school—where no one seems to have any idea who he is.

Something in me refused to acknowledge that anything or anyone had any real power over me.

Mae's new venture is short-lived, and within a month or so, the business fails dismally. She gathers up her children, and returns to Cheyenne.

At some point—perhaps before I went to the orphanage, Mom got a divorce. Now, I'm at the ripe age of just-past-fifteen, and back in Cheyenne with Mom, who is living with some guy in his trailer. She might have been getting food or money prostituting herself. The rooms were nearly empty, and we had to go outside to use the bathroom.

It is amidst this absolute barrenness that Clayton approaches his mother with the intent to coax her away for a private discussion, but she declines. So he decides to have the conversation with her right there. Back they go, into the little house, and Clayton announces, "Mom, I'm going to run away from home, but I want your permission. If someone stopped me, and I could tell them my mom knows where I'm at and I have her permission, then I'm not really a runaway. But, I'm going to leave."

He is making arrangements in advance in case the cops find Mae and begin inquiring, "Why is George Clayton not here?"

She tried to argue about this and that, but I reasoned with her. I told her I could go to Casper, and get a job on a sandbar or something. I didn't have any problem with her. She even helped me pack—Levi's, socks, dress pants, an overcoat. She gave me two-eighty-five to go with the six or seven dollars I'd saved up. She even went with me. Then, I bid her goodnight on one side of town, made it to the other side of town with my pathetic little suitcase, and got on a train.

At 11:00 p.m., as the train pulls into the Casper station, it carries Clayton. He finds one of the bigger hotels in town where a room rents for a-dollar-fifty per night. He knows that he's going to need to become even more frugal if he is to survive, but he tells himself he'll consider such things in the morning, and gets escorted up to his room.

Overlooking the main street, the room contains a bed and an overstuffed chair. Instead of turning down the bed and climbing in, our weary traveler drags the chair over to the window, gets comfortable, and gazes out onto the street until sleep comes for him.

Along about dawn, I went out exploring, and found a storefront with four sets of steel plates where customers set their feet to have their shoes shined. It was called The Hollywood Shine Parlor. This was the beginning of my new life as a shoeshine boy.

On the outside was a sign that read, Hollywood Shine Parlor. Inside was a wiry looking guy named Harry who wore a fedora hat and a gabardine shirt, rolled up so his muscular arms showed like Popeye's. He was a very slick gentleman with his stylish gold watch and his bald head.

Harry was charming and interesting—an open, frank guy you knew was going to give you a square deal. He understood that I was homeless and had just arrived in town. It wasn't long before he agreed to let me help him.

Harry left me in charge of the place, and I was free to make myself at home. I earned five dollars per week—but the real game was the tips. You could make a fortune if you knew how to handle people. I was good at passing the time of day with the customers, adjusting the radio to their liking and admiring their shoes.

With my earnings, I was able to get myself a whitish-gray wool suit from the unclaimed clothes at the cleaners. So, I was a very dapper young kid with good clothing and a nice pair of boots. I also learned to wear a hat. Later when I got to California, I was astonished to see everyone hatless.

I thought very highly of myself, with my nice boots, pretty suit, and a ten-dollar-bill in my pocket. Working at the Hollywood Shine Parlor, I had the sense that everything that had come before had been a prelude. Every twist and turn my life had taken up to now was merely in preparation for this new existence.

For my meals, I ended up with a meal ticket at the restaurant across the street from the cleaners. You paid your money to the restaurant and they gave you a piece of pasteboard worth so much money. For each meal you bought, they clipped a hole in the pasteboard. Eventually, the value of the meal ticket got used up and you bought another. A meal only cost three dollars, and I mean an open-faced tenderloin sandwich with potatoes and gravy!

That's where my money was going—to meals, to the cleaners that kept my suit clean, and to the landlord of a little room I rented up on a hill above the main street. Sometimes I would forego food so I could buy three-for-a-quarter books from the Salvation Army. I read incessantly.

After a while, I met a couple of guys—Orville and Max. Together, we would go to the Five Points area of the city to pick up girls. I also went to the American Legion with Harry, who had been a soldier. I had never joined because I was just a boy, not a soldier, but Harry took me as his guest. It was great to be in the company of adults, ordering liquor, and learning how to flirt with young women.

One night, I ended up on one of the many sofas with a girl. She only let me go so far and I became terribly infatuated with her. She was warm, intimate, friendly, and we both pretended to be a little drunker than we actually were. It was a real high point in my life, going to the American Legion Hall with all these older people. They even had slot machines. There were totally illegal enterprises going on all over.

Even though Harry was kind to me, I found shining shoes to be more and more disagreeable over time. Around the time I started to feel trapped at the Hollywood Shine Parlor, my mother turned up on my doorstep—and moved in with me. She was drunk all the time, and ended up getting picked up and put in jail.

Meanwhile, my brother, Charles Jr., came to stay for a week. He was a military man, in the Air Force at that time. I got it into my head that the time had come to join the military, and I visited an Army recruitment center.

Then, I took the papers from the recruiting station down to the jailhouse, and said to my mother, 'I'm seventeen now. If you will sign these papers, I can join the Army. I think this is what I should do. I'm tired of this life, and I can join the Army under something called The Apple Cheek Plan. After serving three years in the army, I can get a four-year university education at an institute of my choosing—and the Army will pay for it!'

She granted her permission and I was inducted at Fort Riley, Kansas. I had my future all planned out—three years in the military, four years in architecture school, and a nine-to-five job as an architect. I could already draw well enough that if I drew a character like Mickey Mouse or Popeye, you'd know who it was I was trying to depict.

In 1946, when Clayton is seventeen years old, he joins the United States Army. Clayton and the U.S. Army make for a strange alliance, however, as he instinctively distrusts their rules, and they try to break his independent streak.

Every opportunity I got, I did something wrong. I went into the Army a private, and I came out a private. Along the way, I had two stripes on my arm. But, I wasn't easily intimidated. So, any time a situation came up where someone said to me, "Listen, private, you do it right away or you'll talk to the captain," I'd say, "Great! Let me talk to the captain."

After three long years of going against the grain, balking at authority, and doing his best to stay out of trouble, Clayton is finally released. He is a twenty-year-old veteran, preparing to take advantage of the higher education available to him.

I was at Lake Ponchartrain. A huge sea of people was gathered around the edge of the glorious lake. There was a scenic park-like area, with snack bars and a beach. As I was sitting down on my beach blanket, I turned around and saw a very attractive girl sitting nearby. Before long, we were talking. I told her that I was getting out of the Army, and I didn't know where I was going. Her mother joined the conversation, and they told me they were headed back to Montgomery, Alabama, where they lived.

I had been planning to go to architecture school in Berkeley, California, simply because I liked the images Berkeley conjured up in my mind. Berkeley's proximity to Hollywood also appealed to me. But, I figured there was no harm in riding with Mary and her mother to Montgomery. Once there, I planned to bid them goodbye, and then get back on the train for Berkeley. The longer we talked, the closer we became, and the more I was struck by the fact that there was a whole wide world out there.

Clayton's budding romance with Mary—who is a trained acrobat!—leads him to Montgomery, Alabama. Once there, he does not turn around and board the next train to Berkeley, California. Instead, he enrolls in Huntington College, where Mary goes to school. While Huntington is technically a girls' college, they accept male students on the G.I. Bill. Clayton later transfers to the architecture school at Alabama Polytechnic at Auburn.

I had taken—and passed—this certain elite test in the Army. It was a test usually given only to officers. In preparation for the test, I spent a couple of weeks in the library on base, digesting everything I could get my hands on. Afterwards, someone came to the barracks to administer the test to me. He later came back and told me I'd passed. Unfortunately, I wasn't given any written certification of this accomplishment to take with me into civilian life. Instead, my test score went into my file and became a part of my military record. So, I couldn't produce any document to show Huntington or Auburn.

Even as Clayton is perfecting the skills needed for a career in architecture, he is developing his skills as a writer. It starts in drawing class, where he is learning to analyze light, shadow, and depth—and then write about his observations in great detail. This will come in handy later, when he gets a job as a detective for Wilmark, and is required to make observations and then report on what he's observed.

Of course, Fate has something planned for our hero that will prove far more fulfilling than detective work. In the meantime, there is Mary.

For a few months while I was in college, Mary and I were involved in an intense romance. Then her father sensed in me an unwillingness to buckle to his will—and this caused Mary to call it quits with me. At the same time, the three guys I had been bunking with during college suddenly turned on me. The very aspects of my character and personality they'd once admired became the subject of ridicule.

Faced with simultaneous rejection by his college sweetheart and his college roommates, Clayton feels himself slipping into a bleak state of mind, and realizes it's time to make a change. So, he finds himself a suitcase and begins to consider his next move.

I was standing by the highway outside of Auburn, Alabama, wondering where to go from there. I was soured on the university experience, feeling that college was nothing more than a place for kids to be babysat until they could figure out what to do with their lives. I knew that at some point, the government, who was sponsoring my schooling, was going to get wind of the fact that I was leaving the university, but I figured I'd deal with that later. I was ready to get on the road.

~ Transition ~

After traveling for a while, and working at different jobs, I went to visit my sister, Ramona. It was absolutely wonderful to have a chance to be with my sister, and hang out for a couple days.

My sister told me I could find my father in Gillette, Wyoming, so I set out on the road. I found my father living as a bachelor in a one-room place with a couple of cots. He greeted me, and introduced me to his friends as "my son the architect." I watched the compliant way he related to all of them. I was bored to death watching them all josh each other, but I ended up spending a couple of weeks there.

During that time, I drew some plans for a building, and ended up in a discussion with one of my past bosses. I was trying to talk to him about what I considered to be low cost ways to build—a post-and-build system. Every time I started to show him a new aspect of my plans, I ran into a brick wall—I was dealing with northern Wyoming and its extreme weather, but all of my architectural training was for moderate weather.

I happened to meet a guy while I was there. He and I were helping our fathers build a hangar for a tiny plane. We started talking, and he was about to go out to Los Angeles to visit with relatives. He was a rodeo rider, and had been riding bulls and horses in rodeos. He thought he could get a job in California. He was about my age, but was very strong and hard from the life he had lived.

I was growing tired of architecture and liked the idea of California, so together we hitchhiked all the way to Los Angeles. After being all over the country, we ended up in California, amidst lots of cars whizzing past me, and lots of horns honking.

I'll never forget my first driving experience in California, which came later. I pulled into an intersection to find a little old lady with blue hair cranking down the window of her car, and yelling at me, "Get your thumb out of your ass, and drive that thing!" She was this nice, sweet, little old woman, waving me past, as vulgar as hell. That was my introduction to California drivers.

Anyway, I quickly discovered that California was a place of constant change. That's okay with me—I like change. That's the reason I decided to stay here; I look forward to change. Tomorrow—that's the real pull.

It was a very different society than the one you think you're going to find thanks to the imagery you get in movies. It's difficult to make friends or to meet people easily. You can go somewhere two or three nights in a row, and everyone knows you, but a week later, it's a whole new crowd.

It's a world of change—but it's also a world of magic. The guy you've been looking for all your life could be right next to you in the park, looking for his dog—or a date. One day, I saw an actor I recognized from a film. He paused long enough to give me a great big smile. Then, he drove on his way. I believe in the destiny model—something neat in store for you, something that's been planned.

Recently, I was watching the Charlie Rose show. He had on a guest from Egypt. The guy was a substantial looking business type. I was expecting a typical interview, with the appropriate responses. Instead, there was something wonderful between that man and Charlie, a mutual recognition and respect that grew and grew. It turned out that the guy was the richest man in the world. He had brothers who were almost as rich as he.

He made most of his money selling cell phones in the Middle East. He had just expanded to Russia, Indonesia, and China. He planned to go where the people are, and in those locations, the populations are enormous.

Charlie asked him, "To what do you attribute your success?"

The man answered, "God."

"Do you have anything at all to worry about?" Charlie asked.

The man replied, "No. God is going to take good care of me. I have no problem. God likes me."

Me, too. I know everything's cool. It may take some time, and I may wonder, why does God want it this way? But, I have a certain kind of feeling that everything is happening for my own good. When I ask myself why a certain magnificent thing didn't happen then but is happening now, I can usually see that it would have only been a minor success if it happened on my timetable. The fact that it happened later made it a much bigger deal. That's why God screwed it up at that time—because it's much more beneficial now.

No voice is lost. No motion. Every little eddy echoes somewhere. If you knew the initial conditions of the universe, it would be quite possible to calculate exactly where every breath of air is right now. Everything is connected to everything. Nothing is static. It all melds and blends, laps, overlaps, and overlaps again. Believing as I do in the destiny model, I tell myself, Just don't panic! Keep your standards. Don't accept substitutes. What went before will come again.

~ Clarity ~

The guy I'd been hitchhiking with led me to a house in Sun Valley, California, where his relatives lived, and they welcomed me in. Once there, I watched TV, fascinated. It was a black-and-white TV, not expensive, but new. We watched Lawrence Welk and Roller Derby.

That being one of my first viewings, the TV was little more than an oddity to me. I didn't see it as a dramatic instrument. Watching some cranky, creaky guy get up in some plastic booth and read the weather, I couldn't see anything but amusement. I did not see the future. I was not yet thinking that way.

Anyway, I stayed with this guy and his people for about a week or so, diligently applying for jobs. I looked in the paper, saw an ad for Hydro-Air, a company that wanted a draftsman. The location was reachable from Sun Valley. When I filled out the application, I had to answer questions about where I'd been for the past few years. I faked it and bent the truth, but I used all the right names in doing so. My application was accepted.

I now had a job, and was self-sufficient again. I could pay my bills. I lived in a tiny one-room shack in a row of shacks they rented for peanuts. For a mere four dollars—a fragment of my check—I was able to rent the room by the week. I spent no time there except to sleep. During the days, I was working.

While I was at Hydro-Air, I met a man who proved to be an angel to me—Bob Harris Rogers. He was the "chief checker," so every piece of paper had to go through his eyes before it was finalized. He was a kindly man, very patient, and always willing to explain things.

I was given jobs I could execute nicely. One day, I got a call from an officer of the company. They were holding these pieces of paper, saying, "We just received these. We had sent a request to the college you listed *in your application, and they sent back this letter."* He handed me the letter, which said in effect, "Yes, in response to your inquiry, during such and such a period of time, there were four George C. Johnsons enrolled—George Clarence, George Cedric, George Charles, and George Clayton."

The man smiled and filed the letter in the circular file. The letter showed I had been at college, and that seemed to satisfy the company officer. I realized how close I'd come. I was in a high-security-clearance situation, and I was playing a dangerous game. I could not undo the lies I'd told on my application. So, I walked around, from that moment on, with fears of being greeted in the hallway one day by a couple of burly, official looking types, coming to put me in handcuffs.

I used that same application to get a better job at Lockheed. I was going from being a draftsman to a Grade B Junior Engineer. It was a step up in the hierarchy. Within a year, I would be able to drop the "junior" and become a Grade-A Engineer.

It was highly reputable work, and I was getting in on the ground floor. I spent most of my free time at a tavern called the Olive Branch on Hollywood Way near Warner Bros. Studios. I would go, hang out, and eat a sandwich there instead of at a restaurant or café. Before long, I knew everyone there. It was like Cheers, where everybody knows your name.

At work, I could write a good report, and make good use of the language, but it was becoming clear to me that I could not succeed as an architect/engineer. For one thing, the education wasn't really there. I also knew the handcuffs were waiting for me. I'd be thrown in jail if I tried to hang a certificate on the wall claiming I had the license and the education when I didn't. It was a moment of clarity.

To be a writer—that was the life! All my gods were writers. What was it like to be a writer? How did they write these stories? Those kinds of questions had been in my mind all my life. It was not like I'd never written anything. In college, I'd been praised for my ability to write essays.

Valley College was one straight bus ride from the Olive Branch, so at night, when I wasn't at the Olive Branch, I took a course in short-story writing with a man named Professor Korn, an expert in the short-story form. In writing I finally found my true path to success—my destiny.

~ Photo Album ~

In the Johnson back yard (circa 2000)
(credit: Paul Bradford Johnson)

(credit: From the Collection of George Clayton Johnson)

Hand-drawn cartoon
(credit: George Clayton Johnson)

Hand-drawn cartoon
(credit: George Clayton Johnson)

Dark Discoveries cover (circa 2009)
(credit: Jason V Brock)

George and his son, Paul (circa 2007)
(credit: Paul Bradford Johnson)

a) **George and Lola, and their daughter Judy and her husband** (circa 2010)
b) **George**
(credit for both photos: Paul Bradford Johnson)

George (circa 1977) in front of MGM Studios' ad for Logan's Run
(credit: From the Collection of George Clayton Johnson)

George (circa 1977) in front of MGM Studios' ad for Logan's Run
(credit: From the Collection of George Clayton Johnson)

George (circa 1977) in front of MGM Studios' ad for Logan's Run
(credit: From the Collection of George Clayton Johnson)

Photo taken on the set of "The Intruder"—William F. Nolan, George, Charles Barnes, Charles Beaumont, Robert Emhardt, and William Shatner (credit: Carl W. Turk)

George (circa 1977) in front of MGM Studios' ad for Logan's Run
(credit: From the Collection of George Clayton Johnson)

George in the Johnson back yard (circa 2000)
(credit: Paul Bradford Johnson)

George (circa 1977) in front of MGM Studios' ad for Logan's Run
(credit: From the Collection of George Clayton Johnson)

George and Gladys Cooper—during filming of "Nothing in the Dark"
(credit: From the Collection of George Clayton Johnson)

George at Forrest J Ackerman's house
(credit: Christine Lyons (circa late 1960s))

George and Robert Redford—during filming of "Nothing in the Dark"
(credit: From the Collection of George Clayton Johnson)

George, William F. Nolan, Dennis Etchison
(credit: Roy Sanchez)

Book signing with William F. Nolan (circa 2008)
(credit: From the Collection of George Clayton Johnson)

George and William F. Nolan (circa 2008)
(credit: Terry Pace)

George with Dennis Etchison and Richard Matheson
(credit: From the Collection of George Clayton Johnson)

George with author Herbert Simmons and fans
(credit: From the Collection of George Clayton Johnson)

~ Jack Russell ~

At the Olive Branch, I met Jack Russell, an adventurer by trade. Actually, he was a race car mechanic, working out of this little shop, tuning foreign cars for movie people like Keenan Wynn, a famous actor and movie star who would later star in Twilight Zone episodes.

My eyes widened. Wow, he knew Keenan Wynn? That was an important name. I got to know Jack pretty well—and I hoped one day to run into Keenan Wynn.

Jack and I became good buddies. He would come hang out with me in the evenings when I wasn't reading—which I often was, thanks to my library card. Every two weeks, I'd check out ten books. They were big, thick books—literature but also culture.

From books, I was picking up a fantastic amount of information about things as diverse as Greek temples, Corinthian architecture, and antique road shows. When you do this, you're right on top of the game, and know all the right jargon.

At some point when I was in Philadelphia as a young man on the road, there was a very special event being advertised all over town, and it was related to a milestone at the art museum—a fifty-year anniversary or something. The town had gathered a bunch of paintings to exhibit—pieces you wouldn't generally run across at a museum exhibition. There was a Reubens painting that was as big as a house, paintings by Van Gogh, pointillist paintings, abstract paintings, pieces by Miro and Dali. It was quite a collection of distinguished paintings from around the country.

Once it opened to the public, I found buses that would take me there, and I spent a couple of hours wandering the huge halls of the museum, eyed by guards. It was all part of the studies I was pursuing as a way of learning about culture. I also had around the house a lot of books on a variety of subjects—art, fashion, architecture, jewelry. I got to where I could recognize subtleties, like cerulean blue.

This is how I built my knowledge of human culture, especially European culture. I came to the point where I knew the names of all the important composers. Later, when I got to meet Beaumont and his crowd, I knew the jargon, the language, and gave the impression of being college-educated simply because of my vibrations. I had the right glasses, the right haircut.

As I said, I had used the same Hydro-Air application to get a job at Lockheed—but one day I "ditched school" again and left my job at Lockheed. It turned out Jack was also out of work, and the two of us decided to team up. One evening, I looked up Bob Rogers. Jack and I were trying to make our way to his place in the Hollywood Hills, when we got picked up by the police. We looked suspicious, roaming the hills late at night.

They took us down to the station, and I called Bob Rogers. Then the police escorted us to his place. Bob opened the door, and admitting to knowing us. The police explained that they had a warrant. After some confusion, and a nerve-wracking period during which the cops were checking us all out, it was decided that there was nothing wrong with us, and we were free to go. Bob let us stay at his place for a day or two. That cemented my love for him. If he hadn't been there, we would have been booked, no question about it.

After that, Jack and I rented an apartment. Jack schmoozed the landlady, telling her about his job at Competition Motors, selling cars. I tried to join him in selling cars at Competition, but I wasn't cut out for it.

So, I got a job at Wilmark as a store detective. The secretary at Wilmark, to whom all the employees answered, was a young woman named Marilyn Brownstein. She was nice, cute, flippant—if life were a movie, she'd be played by Eve Arden. From time to time, I'd find myself sitting around waiting for an assignment, and I'd talk to Marilyn. She was not my type, but she was a charming, interesting female.

I didn't last too long at Wilmark. After watching a petty thief being railroaded into confessing to a bunch of stuff he hadn't actually done, I quit. But, before I left the job, I got Marilyn's phone number.

I was now unemployed. I went back to my little apartment, and discovered that Jack had gotten some settlement money, bought a little MG and some British looking clothes, and was moving out.

~ LOVE ~

Despite the fact that Clayton—who now goes by George Clayton Johnson, or George—is already aware that Marilyn Brownstein is not really his type, one night he decides to call her and ask her out on a date. Perhaps in this he is guided by what he will come to call "the hidden hand," that elusive hand of fate that unseen, directs the show, for our highest good.

It turned out that Marilyn was seeing someone, and he was there when I called. But, while we were on the phone, I could hear someone in the background giggling, and saying, "Tell him you have a sister!" So, Marilyn told me she had a sister named Lola, and a blind date was arranged. I was twenty-three years old at the time.

Knowing they were on their way to pick him up, George got himself cleaned up, combed his hair, and went out onto the lawn to pick a flower for his date. As they pulled up, they found him standing there with a flower in his hand.

I crowded into the back seat next to Lola's fourteen-year-old brother, Jerry, who had been sent along on the date to be their mother's eyes and ears. I handed the flower to Lola, who was wearing a dark, snug-fitting turtleneck sweater, and a medallion around her neck. She was very pretty—lustrous, even. She didn't think of herself as pretty because she was slightly overweight, and accustomed to playing second fiddle to her sister, Marilyn. Between reciting poems I'd memorized, singing songs, and telling odd jokes, I tried to be the life of the party.

This crowd of five drives around aimlessly, trying to find a suitable destination. At last, someone has the idea to go to the beach. Meanwhile, George's attempts to capture Lola's attention are being thwarted by the fact that she keeps finding ways to get into conversation with her sister's boyfriend, who is driving.

I thought, well, she must be interested in her sister's boyfriend, which is why she came along. So, I said to her confidentially, "You're a very attractive lady. If you're really interested in him, you could get him. Maybe I can help."

She denied being interested in him. The only other explanation was that she was using him as a shield because she didn't like me.

We were driving along the highway by the ocean, pulled over on a bluff, and walked down to the seashore. It was dark, with a little bit of a moon. I said to Lola, "Do you mind if I go swimming?"

When I started taking off my clothes, she turned her back to give me some privacy. The last thing in the world I wanted to do was go swimming, but I had to do something to break the damned spell, whatever it was. The water was cold, up to my waist.

Our intrepid hero endures the freezing cold water as long as he can, and then goes running out of the water—at the exact moment that Jerry lights up an emergency flare, thus illuminating George's naked form.

I'm running for my clothes, which are lying on the sand, and I'm in the headlights of the flare. I was wet and cold, and everyone was laughing at me. It was no longer a private affair.

When we got back in the car, Lola was acting cool—polite and nice, but standoffish. She could see in her brother's eyes that he was going to tell on her for witnessing my nudity. He had made me the object of a joke, deliberately contriving it so that I couldn't get out of the water unseen.

The next day, I picked up my last check from Wilmark and called Lola. "I'm going to the movies," I said. "You're welcome to come along." The reality was, I was only going to the movies if she was going with me. I had caught her off guard, but she agreed to go.

I rode the bus to her house, picked her up, and took her to see a film where Mario Lanza was singing "Be My Love," and making his eyes flash at will.

As we came out of the movies, Lola was acting a little bit cool, and I was trying to be friendly and slightly sarcastic at the same time. We were walking along and talking about life and the deeper meanings of things. She was coming on like a woman of the world, not batting an eyelash when the subject of sex came up.

We got on the bus. I thought, oh, well, another not terribly successful get-together. When we got off the bus, instead of going home, we walked for an hour and talked more and more seriously.

"Do you ever intend to get married?" I asked her. "I can see myself as a family man."

As it turns out, our pair are both dreaming of two children—a boy and a girl. As he and Lola share their visions of the future, George is envisioning ads he's seen of the bright, young American family, decked out in their best clothes, with the father and mother smiling wide as they opened the doors of the family car.

I had that mental image in my mind, and Lola was describing the mental image in her mind. Before we got to her house, we started talking about Paul and Jeanie Wynn—a couple I knew from Hydro-Air. I mentioned the fact that he was a Negro, as they were known in those days. I told her he was a real good friend of mine, and I liked his wife, as well, and would like her to meet them. So, we made arrangements.

The following morning, George picks up Lola and together, they board the bus for Pasadena. When they get within eight blocks of Paul's house, they decide to get off and walk the rest of the way.

As we walked, we talked about life and our dreams and plans. We were taking all this time to get to know each other, becoming more and more comfortable in each other's presence, and enjoying the companionship.

When we got to Paul and Jeanie's house, I thought, perfect—this will be a good test. I needed to see how Lola interacted with them. Any fears or worries I might have had were immediately dispelled when I saw the amazing rapport that was struck up between Paul, Jeanie, and Lola over a Pokeno board. Paul and I both wanted to be writers, and had some good conversation as well.

As we made our way home along the street, we had a much greater sense of connection than before we'd gone to the Wynn's house. Lola was not only honest, but gentle and sincere. She laughed in all the right places, neatly and evenly, and I was impressed that she knew how to help them in the kitchen.

Day by day, we got to know each other more and more. Her mother would turn on the porch lights and call for Lola to come in to bed, as we were sitting in the stairwell a block away, necking.

~ Marriage ~

One day, Lola and I were walking along and I was amusing her by singing "Waltzing Matilda." She stopped and said to me, "Are you going to marry me?"

I said, "I probably will."

I was loath to commit myself further, and that was as much as we discussed that night, but the die had been cast. Now that I'd made the commitment, I was anxious to get it over with and done.

Having an implied commitment to each other, the two go apartment hunting, and quickly find a small place within five or six blocks of Lola's house—which is near Western and Pico in Los Angeles, fifty-four blocks from downtown.

We scraped together enough money to pay for a month's rent. In that apartment, I sat down and wrote a long letter to my mother, which I showed to Lola. "We're going to have a wedding, and I want you to come."

I was aware that I was about to make a serious commitment—like jumping off the edge of a cliff. In most cases, people aren't who you think they are, and it doesn't work out. But, I knew Lola was not lying to gain an advantage and I trusted her. Our relationship was one of growing trust.

I didn't know where to mail the letter to my mother, but I figured I'd eventually get a chance to give the letter to her. I was alone in California with no relatives. That meant I had nobody from my family with whom to share the big day—but it also meant there was nobody with whom to get into one of those arguments that start with the person saying, "But, George, are you sure you know what you're doing?"

I didn't have a white shirt so Lola bought me one. Most of my things had a colored pattern on them so they could get grubby and still look presentable. I brushed up my suit and got myself together.

A well-dressed foursome—George, Lola, Marilyn, and the girls' mother—ride the bus downtown to City Hall. Upon arrival, they enter a room to be questioned by an elderly woman named Ida Mae Adams, whose air of officiousness is emphasized by her judge's robe.

She gave us a very sweet lecture about the sanctity of marriage. She cautioned us against going in before we were ready, pointing out that we were very young, and it was a matter of faith, trust, loyalty, duty, love, commitment, and endurance.

We knew we were ready! Lola's mom and sister were sitting there as Mrs. Adams married us.

Afterwards, we went across the street to a restaurant/bar, and had a celebratory drink together. Then, we rode the bus back to our little apartment. Meanwhile, Marilyn and Lola's mother returned home to put together a little care package for us of plates, saucers, cups, knives, spoons, forks, pans, a platter, salt-and-pepper shakers, and assorted oddities.

Lola's mother and sister brought over the care package and began putting things on the shelves of our tiny triangular room. We had a little chair and couch. Off of that was a little dinette booth and kitchenette with a counter and stove.

The family says their goodbyes, and George and Lola find themselves married and alone together, enjoying their wedding night. Their cups are full of coffee, as they survey their little domicile and contemplate the gravity of the step they have just taken.

A more idyllic spot you can't imagine—this tiny wedge-shaped living space, well appointed, nicely painted, carpeted, and clean. To us, it was a luxurious little space. The two of us sat there, looking at each other.

"Well, now, here it is! My God, we are married!"

And my God, here it is fifty-eight years later. Every day, I marvel over the fact that she and I still cannot enter into a room without entering into a conversation.

As Fate will have it, God will hear their wishes for a boy and a girl, and grant it in the form of their son, Paul, and their daughter, Judy.

~ Home ~

Little did George know when he joined the Army that his time as an enlisted man would pay a huge dividend for him and Lola after they got married. Our newlyweds now discover that, thanks to the G.I. Bill, they are able to buy a house.

During basic training, we were tested to see where we best fit, and I ended up first in the Transportation Corps because I knew how to drive a car, a truck, and a tractor. Before long, I ended up back in Wyoming for training as a telegraph operator, which is sort of like becoming a pickpocket or learning to open locks. It's a unique thing to be able to say I am able to decipher or send a message in Morse Code.

I was in a room with eighteen guys, all bright fellows, and it was then that I became friends with someone by the name of Robert Melson. Each of us was assigned to a little town, and each town was connected by the telegraph line laid during the [American] Indian wars. They were trying to compete with Indian smoke signals and the Pony Express. The Indians could outrun the Pony Express, so people couldn't receive messages.

Flashing messages from mountain peak to peak was faster than smoke signals. That's how they came up with the system. That way, they could switch lights and traffic and understand the way freight was moving across the country. They could make sure the right signals were sent so that the farmer's milk got picked up.

As a station agent on the military railway, our hero is asked where he wants to go at the conclusion of training, and he chooses the Panama Canal. Unfortunately, there is no military railway in Panama.

Robert Melson decided to become a teletype repairman. I saw them repairing teletype machines when they went on the fritz. I was skillful with small tools and the mechanics of old time typewriters, so I was going to join them. Then I saw a drafting section, and decided it would be more interesting. I became a decent cartographer and learned how to make maps. I found out that by being assigned to that duty, I didn't have to go to inspections or certain parades. It was another way of ditching school.

Anyway, Robert Melson wanted us to use the GI bill to our benefit. He wanted to be a doctor and I thought I'd like to be an architect. It seemed noble.

I had initially counted on the opportunities for college afforded to me by the G.I. Bill, but now Lola and I were also going to be able to buy a house! It turned out that the G.I. Bill's real value to me was in the opportunity it afforded me—a writer—to become a homeowner.

Lola works at a nursery school, and between her salary and the coupons the young couple clip, they eke out enough money to buy food to feed their growing family. Yet, they never really have enough money to make their house payment. So, they learn to stall.

Now, the thing with buying a house on the G.I. bill was that they sent you a series of letters when you first became delinquent on your payments, each one brisker than the one before it. I noticed that it was not until you missed your third payment that they sent you a notice of foreclosure. That meant I had four months, with each of the first three notices coming thirty days apart, and then the final thirty-day period during which they could actually foreclose. And, boy did I take advantage of that!

The gas and electricity would get shut off, but those kinds of problems are fairly easy to cure. All you have to do is pay up, and you're back in business. But, curing delinquent house payments requires a more complicated maneuver. The first time we were faced with foreclosure, a certain Mr. Richie made an appointment with us and came out to the house for a little visit.

He saw that we had meager furniture but shiny windows, and he could tell we took pride in our home. He sat with us for two hours, and by the time he left, we had become friends. So, in the intervening years, he came to know my game.

He knew that if I started sliding behind on the house payment, I had a strategy in place. By the time the final notice came, I would find a way to borrow from good friends. I'd get into debt, get the mortgage current again, and start to relax. There were a few instances where things really looked bleak.

~ STRUGGLE ~

I was running my life like a mom-and-pop store, very hands-on, but with little organization. I didn't know what date the electric bill got paid. If someone reminded me it was time to pay a bill, I would mail it. That was my version of organization at that time. I was no good with money; I would blow it on the first damn thing that came along. Lola had a much better handle on our finances, so I turned everything over to her.

Lola knew that my fondest wish was to wake up every morning with twenty dollars I could blow. Maybe I would buy a book, pick up the check if I was out with friends—whatever it might be. To this very day, the first thing Lola does every day is give me a twenty-dollar bill so I will have walking-around money.

I loved to buy Gold Medal novels—twenty-or-thirty-cent books. They totally captured my attention, and I would think, I'd love to be the guy who wrote this! I know I could do this! No one else will believe me. But, if I could just put together a manuscript…

It was a private undertaking, like an artist who begins a painting but doesn't want anyone to see the canvas until the painting is finished. I had no hope that anyone would take me seriously, but I kept telling myself I could do it. And, I had a lot of time in the evenings to write because we had no social life.

Anxiety over finances permeates the following years as George refuses to earn money that he does not earn from writing. He refuses to be the guy who works at the gas station and writes on the side. His training as a draftsman and engineer would allow him to earn a fairly decent wage at a regular job but he isn't interested.

I was trying to train myself to tell people what I did for a living. "I'm a writer! I'm alive. Here I am writing!" That was a big part of it. To backslide, take a part-time job, or have a back door, just in case, would have been to give up my goal. I was already easily dissuaded, and always trying to shake the feeling that I was kidding myself. I wasn't the only one who thought I was kidding myself. People would often ask Lola, "Why does your husband think he's so special? What has he ever done?"

You've heard the phrase "something to fall back on." Well, I didn't want anything to fall back on! I wanted to lock the back door. If there was really a way to do it, why did I need a backup plan?

I understood that the key to success wasn't will, determination, or desire. It was need. When you need to quench your thirst, and there's a bleak desert in front of you, and you've been walking for eight hours, and unless you get that water, you're going to die—that's need. When you need to be a writer, there's something within your psyche that makes you believe you have something to prove.

I was driven to become a great reader first. That's what makes me what I am—the ability to read in lieu of a formal education. If you can read, you can become educated. Throughout the years, I became a better and better reader, and that was part of my clout. I knew the jargon; I knew what things were called. When I started writing, that came through. If I was writing about a detective who discovered a clue, the reader would believe that I really understood things from the inside because I could include the details.

Being a great reader, and knowing the jargon, I therefore have an opportunity to be a great writer. I just have to possess the judgment to know what is worth emulating and copying. I understood that instinctively in the same way I understood about need.

People say that in order to be a great writer, you must have great discipline, and work until four in the morning. Well, I used to think that if I didn't eat every day, I'd die. The most amazing thing I've discovered is that common wisdom is often wrong.

~ Ocean's Eleven ~

George and Lola have their son, Paul (whose sister, Judy, will come later), and a sixty-eight-dollar-a-month mortgage, which is only slightly more expensive than the cost of an apartment. This is astonishingly low, considering they have gone from a one-bedroom apartment to a brand new four-bedroom house, courtesy of the G.I. Bill.

It was a frantic time as we moved, and tried to get some furniture together.

Meanwhile, I was getting together from time to time with Jack Russell, Bob Rogers, and Earl Colbert—a fantastic studio guitarist, who was friends with Barney Kessel, one of the greatest swing-jazz guitarists that ever lived.

The four of us would meet at Dupar's for pecan pie and ice cream, and then I'd bring them back to the house to talk. On occasion, Jack and I would get to talking about the story that would become Ocean's Eleven, and our plans for it. The script was still in its embryo form. We were trying to write it as a novel.

I was telling Jack about a scheme they had in the Republic of Panama—a lottery. I found it fascinating, watching skillful people use inside information to rip off the lottery so they could get the winning ticket to themselves. I thought it would make an interesting story if I could find the characters, the situation, the why, and the how. Out of that idea grew the idea of a super robbery.

I approached it from the standpoint of a blueprint for a crime—if you did it exactly this way, you could do it. I'd make it believable. If they had this; if they did that; if ex-military people, under the leadership of Ocean, contrived this plan to loot several casinos all in one night... They could escape across the desert. It would all be done in a coldly-realistic-no-coincidences kind of game.

They write using Jack's background as a paratrooper. Jack had taken part in the Omaha beachhead—a special series of strikes into Germany, where paratroopers were dropped into specific cities.

He told me a story about how the airborne unit he was part of found themselves involved in this situation in the Alps. The Germans had invented radar, and they had a radar set in the Alps. So, when these huge armadas of bombers crossed Italy and went over the Alps to bomb Germany, the Germans were already in shelters. And, thanks to the radar, the element of surprise was lost, because the Germans had seen them coming.

Jack explained that the Allies wanted to get their hands on that radar. So, they sent in a team of airborne paratroopers, who fell in from the skies and took possession of the radar lab. They dismantled the equipment, took what they wanted, and carried it out on their backs. Then, they had to walk over the Alps and down into France. What the paratroopers could do in wartime, a bunch of guys could do with civilians.

No one in Vegas thought it could happen.

They blew up all the electricals, went in with masks, went straight to the teller's cages, packed everything into huge knapsacks. Then, they hustled out and across the highway to a certain culvert, to wait until everyone was together and they could decide what they were going to do next.

Ocean puts it this way [paraphrasing]: "Where are they? They're ready to do a house-to-house search. They don't imagine highly trained guys like us would put money on our backs in knapsacks, with each man carrying eighty pounds thirty miles at night, to pre-located hideouts with tarps stretched over pulleys. But, we do it in training all the damned time. And meanwhile, they're looking in airports, grilling people in the casinos. So, we walk three hundred miles and cross the only highway leading into Mexico proper. The eleventh man is waiting there with an airplane. There's no one there to bother us."

The plan was designed to be totally credible—except that it was fantasy.

When Jack and Earl and I got together, we were eating ice cream and pie, and the subject came up. I dug out a pile of manuscripts and read a couple of pages. Everyone was amused, and Earl said, "My God, boys, you're onto something here!" Then, Earl said that a friend of his was a television director he'd known for years—Gilbert Kay, who'd been an assistant director on many Hollywood movies, and finally got an opportunity to direct.

Earl asked if he could bring Gilbert over to my place for some pie. I notified Jack, and before we knew it, there were four of us in the room, and Lola. I was reading out loud the story I'd put together, with me and Jack stopping to explain the plot. We ended up doing a pitch on it with the reading.

Gilbert Kay became excited, saying that it should be a screenplay, not a novel. And, he told us he would show us how to write a screenplay. He saw himself directing this movie that was, as yet, unwritten.

We ended up meeting with him several times. Gilbert started talking to Samuel Furman, the son of the owner of Furman Furs in Beverly Hills. It seemed that Mr. Furman was interested in finding a good place to invest ten thousand dollars of his money, in exchange for ten-percent ownership. It seemed like it could come in handy to have a businesslike financial guy behind us, one who owned part of our action.

We took the ten thousand dollars, and formed Matador Productions. We became a foursome—me, Jack, Gilbert, and Earl—and rented a little office. We gave ourselves a hundred dollars a week as salary, and went to work.

They turn it out, page by page, with George as the draftsman lettering it all out by hand. He writes in especially large letters, covering as many pages as he can, in an effort to feel industrious. They go through the plot, section by section. George is the final judge as to what gets written down.

During this time, Bob Rogers had his house at the top of Laurel Canyon, Earl Colbert rented a cottage down on Willow Glen in Laurel Canyon, and I began to see the attraction of Laurel Canyon. There was a coffee bar café there, a real estate office, and a few other establishments clustered around. We would sit on the porch of the coffee house. People I began to think of as "the faces" would show up—wannabe writers, directors. Earl's place became kind of our headquarters when we weren't going to the office.

Gilbert started talking to us about Peter Lawford, whom he knew from when he was the assistant director on a Peter Lawford/June Allison film. Anyway, he thought Peter Lawford might be interested in our story. So, now we'd finally cobbled together a screenplay, and

Gilbert had taken it off to get it typed up. We were waiting for him to get it back to us.

He had become our leader, and we'd all succumbed to his charm and authority. With Gilbert out of the picture now, I had to forego haircuts, and scrounge around for quarters to get to Laurel Canyon, where I would wait at Bob's or Earl's for some news from Gilbert.

While they are waiting, George discovers that Gilbert has taken the script to the Preminger Agency.

I had developed my own longhaired beatnik style, and one day, dressed in that garb, I walked into the Ingo Preminger Agency, and announced to the girl at the front desk, "I'm one of the guys who wrote Ocean's Eleven!"

She gestured towards a pile of scripts that said Ocean's Eleven on them, and when I opened them, my name wasn't on them! By this time, a door opened, and Malcolm Stewart, an agent of some renown, walked out. Malcolm seemed confused as I tried to explain myself.

"But," he said, "I was under the impression Gilbert wrote it!" He started backing away from me.

Gilbert was a card-carrying member of the Writer's Guild, so when we'd registered the script, he had been designated as the writer. Now that the writing was done, Gilbert had dismissed me, and Jack, too. It turned out that he'd told Malcolm Stewart that he thought he'd have better luck promoting the script with his own name on it. He figured that his credibility would sell it. Gilbert had also promised Earl a part in the picture, so Earl was seeing Gilbert as a future employer.

Well, Malcolm let Gilbert get away with it. Instead of getting indignant along with us over what Gilbert had done, Malcolm just lay back and let Gilbert do what he was going to do. He didn't want to get involved.

Jack and I felt that Malcolm was loyal to Gilbert, and we could see we were getting shafted. We were not going to stand still for it. Meanwhile, Gilbert had given a copy of the script to Peter Lawford, who read it and made an offer to buy it. He sent the offer through his agent to Gilbert.

We were now at swords' points, with no one trusting anyone anymore. I am an hysteric, and my attitude was, "To hell with it!" Gilbert had arbitrarily changed the whole story around just to make a sale, and I said, "Screw you! I wouldn't want to work with you, anyway!" So, there was all of this argument stuff seething between us on the one hand, and on the other hand, there was this offer.

If we signed it, we'd get away from each other—but we'd be selling all of our future rights. It was a merciless agreement, and today I'd turn it down, and get a better deal in a counteroffer.

I had to foreswear all future children, so to speak. Now, Matador Productions had been crushed, and we'd sold all of our rights to Peter Lawford. We got a check from Kathleen Kennedy. Then, Lawford involved Sinatra, and the rest is history.

We sold it with the expectation being that it would be made soon—that season or the next season. Time went by, and we didn't hear about it.

The original was rewritten five times before they made the picture. Some of the best people in Hollywood were involved. Richard Green was the president of the Writer's Guild of America. Daniel Fuchs was a blacklisted writer. Finally, they ended up with Harry Joe Brown and Charles Lederer. Then Lewis Milestone rewrote it. Richard Benedict was rewriting it on set. Everyone had a chance at it.

We were writing the opening scene in such a way that they've already got the money, and they're walking across the desert, talking. Then we flash back to the beginning. But, it wasn't done that way. It started in a casino, with Ocean making his plans to gather together his people.

On the film set of *Ocean's Eleven*, George interviews Dean Martin, Sammy Davis Jr., and Frank Sinatra. He is granted access to the set not as the story writer—which he is—but as someone on assignment for *Playboy*.

I was lurking around as this inquiring reporter, and eavesdropping on conversations. When Sinatra noticed me, he asked me who I was and I told him. "I wrote the original screenplay for the film, and I'm here for Playboy." I was totally intimidated. I explained to him, "I believe this could be a book. I could do a novelization of Ocean's Eleven if I had permission. Could you give me the rights to do the novelization? I sold everything when I sold the screenplay." The whole time I'm talking, I'm looking at him, thinking, damn, his eyes are blue!

Ol' Blue Eyes is perfectly polite and pleasant in his demeanor with George, but explains that his hands are tied. "You'd have to speak with my agents," he says, writing down the phone number for Rogers & Cowan Public Relations, and handing it to George.

I found a phone, and talked to a nice young man at Rogers & Cowan, who told me, "It's too goddamn bad because I'd like to keep Frank happy, but I just made a deal with Cardinal books, a subsidiary of Pocketbooks." I went back to the set, brokenhearted.

Despite its disappointments, Ocean's Eleven is a turning point for our young writer. For it marks an irrevocable decision.

Lola and I put our heads together and realized it wasn't a totally insane idea for me to devote all my time to writing. Because, even though the money I made on Ocean's Eleven was far less than I should have made, it was more than we'd ever expected.

When the movie finally came out, the Group went down to this famous film house in Hollywood where it was playing. As I sat in the audience, I saw the incredible way Saul Bass had done the credit, taking "Written by George Clayton Johnson and Jack Golden Russell" and making it into one long sentence that read "Story: George Clayton Johnson and Jack Russell" and stretching that across the movie screen from edge to edge.

To have Beaumont and the others sitting around me was very trippy, but considering who they were, it was hard to be too puffed up.

I got the WGA nomination for best screenplay, listed as one of five comedies being nominated. In the hotel bar where we were having the WGA Awards banquet, I got a chance to see my Twilight Zone episode, The Prime Mover.

~ The Group ~

After Lola, Charles Beaumont becomes one of the most important figures in George's life.

Beaumont was my first professional writer. He had a book out, The Intruder, which was made into a movie. He also had a collection of superb tales called The Hunger and Other Stories. He was getting a five-hundred-a-month retainer from Playboy just for a first look at his work!

I was thinking of him the other night, and asking myself what it was about him that had such a magnetic hold on my imagination.

Chuck had a way of giving you his attention. There was something in those eyes, something that drew my respect. That quality in him made me rise up to my highest level, fearful of appearing a jerk, cautious of overstatement or boasting or exaggeration. It was the sense that, "Now daddy is watching you! You don't do these things!" I had the desire to be his equal and prove myself intellectually. I became aware that I'd been guilty of glittering generalities, of avoidance of the specific when I didn't know something.

He was a great salesman, affable and easygoing. But, perhaps his greatest influence lay in his intellectual honesty. He was willing to call a spade a spade, and be wrong if he was wrong. He'd say, "Thank you for clearing that up for me."

On my part, I became the fellow whose basic role was to support his act. I was like the thug in the movies. If anyone made a move on him, I'd trip them up. He learned to trust me because I was not trying to get laughs at his expense, and not trying to use him to gain notoriety.

He had an imaginative interest in a whole lot of things, and I often went along with him to play bumper cars, or to a strip joint, where we would applaud and leave tips. Sometimes, we'd just go see some film he wanted to see. It was a wonderful experience for me.

Charles Beaumont is also introducing George to some of his closest friends—people like John Tomerlin and William F. Nolan. Along with Beaumont, these two had been part of something they called The Group.

I found myself immersed in The Group, and John, Bill, Chuck, and I often found ourselves together. Visits with The Group often included my wife, Lola, Chuck's wife, Helen, John's wife, Wilma, and their children. We were all family men, with strong identities as fathers. And we all had much in common in terms of age and interest. But there was clear knowledge that Chuck had climbed the tree—he was selling his work to TV; he had all the right agents.

In that ring of writers, I was learning the ropes, becoming more "ringwise." I was observing how they spoke to secretaries, how they handled their files and notes. I learned that a writer saves all scrap paper—he doesn't tear it up and throw it away. He might find that something he is writing almost works, and then he has to return to his notes. I was learning those sorts of things from my encounters with The Group.

Once I'd met and become part of The Group, I began to think of my life as divided into two parts—the years that came before meeting The Group, and everything that happened afterwards.

The camaraderie and companionship of those in The Group became invaluable to me. The Group grew to include Richard Matheson, Ray Bradbury, O.C. Rich, and a bunch of surrounding people like Ray Russell, the editor of Playboy magazine, and Frank M. Robinson, the editor of Rogue magazine and a novelist in his own right.

This was the most enlightening period of my life. I was at the peak of my powers, growing into my prime. I could easily go without food, and was known to voluntarily fast once in a while, just to keep myself agile and trim. There were story conferences, conventions, and panel talks. There was even a film made about me called Dreamspinner. I was known as a friend of Charles Beaumont's, but also as a wild dog who wouldn't stop being a beatnik.

This period of time was formative. My association with Beaumont had led to me knowing how to get a story submitted to The Twilight Zone. I was cruising along, making connections, learning the diligence that goes into every endeavor in the game.

Thanks to The Group, I never had to climb the ladder from box boy, so to speak, to store manager. The credits I was adding to my resume were just esoteric enough that I fit in easily with The Group—and the fans.

While learning about movie deals—what should and shouldn't be in contracts—I made all manner of mistakes. I learned about the end game from watching Charles closing deals, arguing with directors and producers. I began to see the process like a game of chess, with a beginning, middle, and end game. I started to understand that you could have good game in the beginning and middle, but it would all fall apart if you didn't carry through on the end game.

~ ALL OF US ARE DYING ~

George Clayton Johnson is trying to write stories, and has his eye on television. When he finally gets a good draft of his story, *All of Us Are Dying*, he sends it over to Ray Bradbury, his mentor.

Ray wrote back, praising it, but said, "I think you need a bigger ending." So, a day or two later, I took the story over to Charles Beaumont and showed it to him. When I told him what Ray had said, Chuck said, "He's right!" Then, Beaumont wrote the last four lines for me verbally.

I didn't yet have an agent, but Jerry Sohl's agent was prepared to talk to me. I showed him the story, All of Us Are Dying, and he took it into another room to read it. When he came back out, he said, "I like it, and I want to submit it. But the title is wrong." He suddenly had an inspiration, scratched out my title, and wrote in The Four of Us are Dying.

I was happy to have him submit it, which he did shortly thereafter, to Twilight Zone producer Buck Houghton. There was ecstasy around here for quite a while.

It was that manuscript that Jay Richard at Famous Artists—the head of the TV department—sold. Once it had been bought, I was approached by The Ashley Steiner Agency, the people connected with The Twilight Zone. Since Jay Richard had thought me too young and inexperienced to sign, this agent from Ashley Steiner agreed to meet with me. His name was Ben F. Conway.

The two hit it off and Ben says he will represent George. Slowly but surely, George and Lola start to recover financially, as money begins trickling in to make the house payment. Things are really opening up, and George is getting more of a sense of himself, now that he has some credits to his name.

I now knew there was a potential market for me, but by hanging out with Charles Beaumont and friends, I never got too full of myself. If you're hanging around with people with dozens of prestigious credits, you can't get puffed up. They were veterans, and the doors were just starting to swing open for me, as I began to write teleplays.

Meanwhile, I was very interested in doing more television. It became very important to me—what would I show this guy? What would intrigue him? What would Rod Serling consider "true Twilight Zone?"

~ Execution ~

George immediately goes to work on *Execution*, which Rod Serling buys. The story, which deals with the theme of divine retribution, is written off the enthusiasm of the first sale and the awareness that there is a possible open door for him at *The Twilight Zone*.

It was based on an idea that always fascinated me—the time machine. I think of it like a temporal distorter, a scoop shovel. You reach this distorter back into time, scoop up something, bring it back into the future, and calibrate it. H.G. Wells was the first one to let you hear about a temporal distorter, and it was astonishing, marvelous, and new in its time.

A lonesome cowboy goes back and gets a true piece of the cross on which Jesus was crucified, or one of thirty pieces of silver that represented Judas' payoff for betraying Christ. He discovers that there is a remarkable curse on those items, and a strange fate linking to that betrayal. A group of people want to loot the world, collecting all the great treasures of the past—that's the obsession behind this device.

That became a cowboy, hung for his crimes, who somehow got picked up by the scoop shovel and carried into the future or the present. I liked the idea of a savage cowboy from the past finding himself in an age where everything around him is alien. He touches the wall and lights come on. Boom! A window shade comes clattering down. He wonders how he got there and what happened to the lobby of the hotel he was in.

All of it—tall buildings, automobiles, TV's, a machine that goes down the street carrying happy children—everything is an astonishment. He's not from that world, so everything seems completely unreal and imaginary.

Thinking about all this, I was trying to fashion a tale that would intrigue Rod Serling, knowing his dark, sardonic take on things. They hadn't done anything like this—a time machine distorter. I started exploring this idea in every possible way, and piling up dozens of notes of different kinds of stories in which you had a temporal distorter.

One idea I came up with ended up being a different story of mine—The Edge of the World. That was based on this question: what if our cowboy comes back with a piece of a broken boat made of ancient wood, with the name "Santa Maria" on it? What if he reaches back into time and interrupts the voyage of Christopher Columbus, comes to the edge of the world, and plunges over? There you have The Edge of the World.

Anyway, I was thinking about how time is paradoxical and mysterious, and realized I could do a fresh, new time machine story unlike the others if I could only think of the paradoxical difference that was different from what someone else had done.

Execution had sufficient pizzazz. It was written as a short story, but it was really an outline for a TV script. I was still trying to learn how to do a teleplay. I wanted to tell enough that it became photogenic fiction, going from scene to scene, from setting to setting, and always with something three-dimensional in the reader's mind. Visual, visual, visual, place after place—that's the nature of the outline. It doesn't tell you what they said; it tells you what they did.

I had the cowboy being seized by the noose, and encountering the TV set. I fashioned the story around the idea that he is given a chance to be saved in this new world, to renounce his evil ways. Will a man, when given an opportunity, renounce his evil ways? No, he's the same old guy, and he's going to get hung again by the same noose. The story is based on the philosophy of how-they-act-is-how-they-are and what-they-do-is-what-they-are-going-to-do.

Anyway, I turned Execution in to Rod Serling or Buck Houghton, and I received a message: They were buying it and sending me a contract and a check!

The original title was The Hanging of Jason Black. In Rod's adaptation, the character became Joe Caswell. Rod looked at my key elements—there's the ideas, the settings, the circumstances, the possible effects—and then his fertile mind went to work. He looked at my story as an armature, then renamed the characters and changed their motivations.

My story wasn't television yet. It was a short story, sure, but the psychological stuff had to be turned into action, and the high rise into a storefront.

I had one of the greatest teachers. Rod wrote some incredibly good dialogue, a few key sentences that showed the characters' states of mind, and a few exchanges that became a little conversation. I watched what Rod would do, where he would take what I'd done, how he would stack things up in a different way. I was learning as I went.

When my show finally aired, it was now called Execution and starred Albert Salmi. I got to visit the set while they were shooting.

I saw the script and marveled at the changes. What an education it was! I could see my story in there, and what Rod had done with it, and I thought, My God! How clever! I realized what an unenviable job Rod—or Buck—had. Just as an outline is somewhat different from a script, a script is really different from the broadcast.

There I was, watching the episode, watching the actors, and the hanging scene came up. I was very impressed with Rod. As the script was enacted, it had incredible power, and strong solid lines. Rod really caught the whole dark moodiness of it. Everything Rod was famous for was captured in that story.

Albert Salmi, meanwhile, was an amazing man, a method actor from the Stella Adler tradition, I think. It was great getting an opportunity to meet him. We went to this little bar/restaurant located near M-G-M, and we were all eating. We had only one hour before we had to get back to the set. I was trying to get to know Salmi, but he was sitting there holding his fork and knife in the most awkward, almost swine-ish way, and paying no attention to me whatsoever.

I wondered what the hell was happening. He didn't seem at all interested in making my acquaintance. Then, it hit me—that was Joe Caswell, not Albert Salmi! He was staying in character so that when he played the next scene, he would be filled with anger. Lola was there with me.

I got a chance to talk with the director, but mostly I stood aloof, watching it all, trying to learn from what I was seeing, and trying to look like I belonged. I was just a neophyte.

~ Companionship ~

John Tomerlin, Bill Nolan, Chuck Beaumont, and I became the Four Musketeers and kept The Group together. Unless one or more of us was caught in a deadline, we often found ourselves free, with nothing to do. So, late at night, one or two of us would go pick up the others.

The next thing we knew, we'd find ourselves listening to the hi-fi in the middle of the night, or whatever Chuck wanted to do. He inspired us all to think sideways rather than logically forward. Our discussions had mostly to do with our accomplishments and ambitions—what we all had to say about what everyone was working on.

I was not yet the glib television writer I am today. I was much more introspective and guarded. I didn't want to give away any of my weapons. I didn't want to confess that I didn't have a car, that I'd lived in an orphanage, that I wouldn't be able to pay for my own coffee.

I had a sense that I needed to just lay low and fit in. At the same time, I was set on being a nonconformist. I would engage in intellectual arguments but I never brought anger into it. A guy doesn't mind you arguing if you don't bring anger to the discussion.

I wasn't afraid to say I believed in ghosts—or the tooth fairy.

They'd challenge me, "Come on, George, you can't really believe this!"

Or, I'd say, "If they want to win this war, get rid of Roosevelt and put Clark Gable in there!" I grew up with those images in my mind, and saw myself as Bogart.

Why not? It appealed to me. It was magical. It worked beautifully and on some level, it was a deep truth—like music. Some poet said, "Beauty is truth and truth is beauty." I always believed that if a thing was beautiful, why wouldn't it be true?

If The Group was some place, I wanted to go, too, and I would try to find a way to get there. Sometimes that meant hitchhiking to get there, and depending upon the kindness of strangers to buy me a cup of coffee. I would never beg or whine, but if someone offered, I'd say, "Sure, I'd love a cup of coffee."

~ CONVENTIONS ~

At WorldCon I met writers and became a part of the group called The Fictioneers. When the event—which was to be held at the Alexandria Hotel in Los Angeles—rolled around, Charles Beaumont was invited. He was going to be raffling himself off as a dinner companion, with the proceeds going to charity.

Beaumont was allowed to bring a couple of guests. So, he suggested he take Lola and me with him. We got ourselves gussied up in our best outfits, and off we went. Richard Matheson was a guest of honor, and Robert Bloch the master of ceremonies.

Over the three-day weekend, thousands of people attended, and I became aware of the fact that there were twenty or thirty big-name editors, as well as luminous sci-fi writers in the hotel—people like Paul Anderson, H.L. Gold, John W. Campbell, A. E. Van Vogt, Forrest J. Ackerman, Sam Mines. I later met some of these same people at the Fictioneer Convention.

That's also where I met my good friend, Jerry Sohl, a fellow Twilight Zone writer, and through me, he met Beaumont. I would later write the afterword for his Collected Twilight Zone Scripts book.

This place was teeming with people in capes and costumes, looking eerie, and for Lola and me, it was a first. We had arrived there with Chuck, who got quickly pulled away, and now Lola and I were lost at sea. There we stood, trembling, feeling insecure, and trying not to stand out too much. All of a sudden, down the staircase comes this handsome fellow who was my age or maybe a little bit older. He looked like a newcomer, himself.

We were standing at the foot of the stairs as he descended with a curious expression on his face. So, I said, "Hi, I'm George!" and he said, "Hello,

I'm Jerry!" (Jerry Sohl.) Now there were three of us, which made us feel less awkward. We started moving towards wherever there was interest, and Jerry tagged along with us. In this way, we became convention mates.

Jerry was with us when we went into the banquet, and with us when Beaumont would join us and then leave again. He was with us to meet Robert Bloch and Richard Matheson. The assumption was that you'd written things or you wouldn't be there. This event culminated in a fast friendship with Jerry, and his friendship with Beaumont.

We were in rooms stuffed with people sitting on beds, leaning against the walls, talking, smoking, and refreshing themselves with the makeshift bar laid out on the hotel dresser. I found myself transported to the center of everything important happening with science fiction, of which I was a devotee.

I was awed by this leaderless society, and wondering where they'd been all my life. I realized, I am in the presence of greatness here! It was a very holy thing, to see these people not in competition, but helping each other. They spent all their time lionizing each other. I was watching a very special breed of cat.

Part of my profession as a writer is to keep up to date on fandom—which is a unique social phenomenon. These people are the keepers of the soul. They are a rapscallion crew, and over time, they have become more important academically and socially. Sure, I've had an influence on them over the years, but my heart is where their heart is, and if I were not me, the Fictioneer, I'd be glad to be one of them.

My heart lies with the fans, with the people who love the Wolfman and Lon Chaney—the loners. These nerds, who never got accepted, gather together for warmth and to share the thing they have in common—their imaginations. You can be in league with this group while contradicting them. Because fandom is a leaderless society, no one is in charge, which means that no one can throw you into exile.

The conventions themselves have always allowed me to be visible and active—"There is George, still writing!" People wondering about what I was up to could say to each other, "I recently saw him interviewed…or photographed." That has always given me a sense of being a working writer. Even if I am at a convention, I am building my brand name.

The fans became my vehicle for learning to speak to groups, becoming comfortable in public, developing the ability to send forth my authority into a room before entering. Whenever I was around the fans, I had the sense that the attention was coming from the future, coming from a world that was aware of us here on earth. Like a secret camera, recording our every gesture, assessing our merits.

Over the following years, I must have attended a hundred and fifty conventions, but this one introduced me to this family, and I got to know the biggest names on a first-name basis. I could write a separate chapter on what each of these men meant to my life, but suffice it to say that collectively, they made me feel like I was getting somewhere. To be in the presence of those people, with their support and acknowledgment, and discover they were just real people, not slick, standoffish professionals, was exhilarating.

I recently received a call from the founder and chairman of San Diego's ComicCon convention, letting me know that, while going through old photos, he came across a picture of Timothy Leary, Theodore Sturgeon, and me. I remember sitting on that panel with them, discussing the future.

~ Fictioneers ~

George will be in the process of making his breakthrough in television when Charles Beaumont tells him about an upcoming meeting of the Fictioneers, and agrees to take him to the Fictioneer Convention, being held in the upstairs banquet room of a restaurant that is walking distance from Schwab's on Sunset.

This group of writers had in common the fact that they all wrote for pulp magazines—a penny per word, a quarter per word. They would write western stories, detective stories, spy stories, foreign intrigue stories, one right after another. They considered themselves a club of writers that could make up stories on demand. This gave them the reputation and the air of professional story makers depended upon to give you a good yarn. All you had to do was ask, and they'd reply, "Do you have anything particular in mind?"

Between themselves and the magazine editors, they would lay out the plot. They would write to spec, for a price, within a specific timeframe. These were professionals who respected each other, and understood the difficulty of their task. In those days, if editors had forty-two western magazines to fill with stories, they had a coterie of people that could work for them. Now, we have forty-two television hours—or whatever the number—to be filled instead of magazines. The producer is your editor.

Ed comes to me and says, "George, we've done a pirate story, and last week we did a Medusa story, and now we're thinking about a pickpocket story. Or, a King Midas type of story, where a guy touches things and they turn to stone or to gold. So, he's got to be careful. If he touches something, you're doomed. Can you do it?"

Then, I'd ask, "Who is your hero?"

Being a Fictioneer was a very vivid identity, a handle. My God, I wondered, could I be a Fictioneer? Could I make a whole career out of it and be like Jack London or Edgar Rice Burroughs? Could I become that kind of person? Could I come up with enough ideas to get enough experience?

That was a longed-for ambition, but I saw no way to realize it because the very magazines I was writing for were dying or about to be gone over the horizon. Just as I was thinking it was too bad to see these magazines go, television was rising from the ashes.

This Fictioneer Convention was an opportunity for me to find myself rubbing shoulders with terribly important men, like A. E. Van Vogt and Robert Bloch. These fellows had, for years and years, been dealing with this world where I was only a beginner.

Ray Bradbury was the main speaker, and I hung on every word. At the conclusion of the meeting, we went downstairs, where Bradbury was being lionized and led through the crowd. He found a place at the open bar, where he sat, surrounded by people, and ordered a drink.

I was at his elbow. Here was my opportunity to speak to Ray Bradbury. He was a beacon of light, and I saw in his electric methods the salvation of the literary world. Everything he had done had stunned—and intimidated—me.

~ Ray Bradbury ~

As it so happened, I had just finished reading *Icarus Montgolfier Wright*. So, I told Ray, "I just finished *Icarus*, and my God, Almighty! It would make a wonderful animated movie…" In the course of that conversation, I suggested to him that I could easily visualize how it might be illustrated, and I'd love to write a script for *Icarus*.

Ray was very avuncular, and clapped me on the shoulder, saying, "Go ahead with the writing! Write regularly—just before you turn out the lights. If you write one page a day, one simple page, and set it aside, you'll have a script by the end of thirty days." He was trying to encourage me in this wild idea I told him about while he happened to be getting a drink.

When I got home, I immediately went to work on it, and within three days, I had something I felt good about. The saying yes, the exchanging of contracts—all of that stuff was almost immediately in play. Then Ray took the script, ran it through his typewriter, changed things, and put a new title on it, with the credit of "By Ray Bradbury and George Clayton Johnson based upon a story by Ray Bradbury."

There was his credit! By putting his name on the script, he made it so valuable. I went out like a super-agent, showing it to my friends, some of whom had power in the business. Connections were made. A man named Herb Klynn, who had split from a big agency over artistic differences, had gone out and formed Format Films. I managed to get the property to that company.

Next, Klynn wanted to meet with Ray Bradbury and me. At the meeting, Klynn laid out his plan. It would be seventeen minutes long—a semi-animated film. Joseph Mugnaini—an artist who worked on Ray's book covers—would do the artwork on this animated film. It would be largely a matter of taking drawings and paintings, and superimposing them on each other.

Joe was the head of the Art Department at Otis Art Institute. He was an artistic giant, famous with Bradbury. He had a most remarkable style, and taught a number of celebrity students. Every year, he would take a group of students midway between Ensenada and Tijuana for a party. These were huge gatherings, and I joined everyone, loafing around, drinking beer, and dancing at a cantina.

There were three thousand watercolor sketches, out of which we picked three hundred to draw as cellophanes (cels). Finally, we ended up with the film. It took two years from the time I gave that script to Ray. This was my second credit, but it would not improve my standing until the film was seen.

The movie would be sold and distributed, and the film profits divided into eight shares, split among Ray, Joe the artist, and me, with Joe getting the lion's share of the profits, since his artwork comprised the lion's share of the labor. In order for it to be eligible for Academy consideration, the film had to be shown for a certain amount of time. It was booked into a Westwood theater and shown alongside an art film called Phaedra.

We all went down to the showing. It was great seeing it in a movie house on a large screen, and I thought it was gorgeous. The whole world of Icarus was juicy and odd.

At the end of that year, our film of Icarus Montgolfier Wright was nominated for an Academy Award in the animated shorts category! Also in the category was John and Faith Hubley's movie, The Hole, and they won the Oscar. But, it was so validating to be nominated, and get to go to the Academy Award ceremony.

~ Star Trek ~

As Charles Beaumont grew older, he started to get us to help him from time to time. One time, he had an appointment to talk to people about doing Wanted: Dead or Alive with Steve McQueen, and he didn't have a story to take them. So, I told him a story—and they bought it from him. Then, he bought it from me for six hundred dollars. I wrote it and later got credit, but not at the time. It was the fans who gave me credit.

I loved the whole idea of being considered a Fictioneer. It was wonderful, corny, nostalgic, like being an astronaut. I knew that the Fictioneers were a society of real writers.

George meets Gene Coon (along with Gene's wife, Joy, a wonderful artist) at meetings of The Fictioneers. George's meeting with Gene Coon proves to be fortuitous, indeed, resulting in George's introduction to *Star Trek*'s Gene Roddenberry. Six scripts are purchased and filmed in preparation for *Star Trek* going on the air. Now, the executives at NBC just have to select which of the six will provide the viewing audience with their first taste of the series, becoming the pre-pilot episode of *Star Trek*.

TV was just switching to color, and as a result, there was a lot of brainstorming and discussion in the executive offices at the network as to how best to use color. There just happened to be tons of color in Star Trek, tons of primary colors.

As they were preparing to release Star Trek, they got together and decided, "The actual show is a week away. Meanwhile, why don't we take one of these six and stick it into that slot so that people who are normally watching The Fugitive get a splash of this highly colored show!"

For some reason, they chose my episode, The Man Trap. It was only years later, when I was talking to Herb Solo, that I found out one of the major reasons for the NBC brass choosing my episode over the others.

He told me, "By going with yours, we were able to open the series with the crew getting aboard the transporter device and beaming down to the planet. By letting the audience watch the transporter in action, and letting them see the crew materialize and dematerialize, we were saved from having to try to explain it."

Another factor was that my episode took place on an alien planet—not just aboard the Starship Enterprise. Mine was more comprehensive and broader in scope. Anyway, Star Trek ended up having two pilots before it ever went on the air—my episode and the actual pilot!

That I would end up writing the premiere episode for Star Trek made sense to me. After all, I always believed that the world of the spirit was the only one worth paying attention to. When you dream, it's your spiritual self that perceives things. When you die, the world "out there" goes away, and your spirit is all that remains.

I don't believe that death brings an end to the parade. Nothing vanishes or goes away. There is a world waiting beyond this material world. Knowing it's out there is what allows me to think up my stories. I can literally see other worlds come into my mind.

~ Route 66 ~

During this period with The Group, I realized I had to broaden myself as a television writer. Route 66 really appealed to me. I liked the story of two young men who set out to make their fortunes. One has inherited a special Chevy Corvette, and they cruise from town to town on their adventures.

I could envision myself as those two young men, playing those roles. I could also come up with a story. That's the essential thing with television—they have half a story…a transporter, a Mr. Spock, a Captain Kirk. That's their story. What they need are the connective materials in the middle. I was good at supplying that, so I got a job writing for Route 66.

I wrote a story of a dying desert town that had not been included on the route when the freeway went past. Despite the fact that the tourist business has died, and the mining business has died, the townspeople don't want to leave. They believe the town could have a revival if they could get the freeway running through their town—but they need enough money to build the freeway. So, they take all the money out of their mattresses and give it to the town banker and a local two-bit gambler.

The two men are sent to Reno to gamble the money. They leave with one suitcase filled with money, and one empty. The hope is that they will return with two suitcases full of money. The banker is played by Edward Andrews and the two-bit gambler by Walter Matthau. The townspeople want the town gambler to do the gambling; they don't trust him to handle the money. They send the banker along to handle the money.

The suits at Route 66 liked my idea and put me to work on it. My idea was based on something I'd read where a guy shows up at a big casino with two suitcases—one full and one empty—and either he will lose all his money or fill the second suitcase. So, I said to myself, that's a very good idea, and I worked out a notion that was eventually called Eleven the Hard Way.

I went to Reno to watch them shoot. It was a very nice little show, and I got a chance to spread my wings.

~ Leverage ~

I was becoming a Rod Serling forger.

I considered Execution to be wisdom fiction because it had a great message. After that, I sat down and wrote Sea Change. I copied the way Rod's characters would talk, and tried to come up with the kind of characters that would really look good on screen—mangy, demoralized, pathetic. An old lady and old man who are about to die are being offered new bodies, but they can only afford one.

The Twilight Zone buys Sea Change right away—and then, to George's great disappointment, they give it back. The show's sponsor, General Foods, takes issue with a certain element in the story.

They said to Rod, "Look, the idea of someone getting their hand cut off over the dinner table is gross!" They thought the image was too dark.

By returning to Rod Serling and Buck Houghton the money he's been paid for Sea Change, George gains leverage for A Penny for Your Thoughts.

On this one, I would end up telling them they couldn't have the story unless I wrote the script. I knew they owed me for having given me back Sea Change.

As George is perfecting his trade by observing the way that Rod takes his ideas and adds to them, George realizes that his ideas are his contribution.

They were like the metal rod in a statue. I provided the armature and Rod provided the statue. That's the true nature of a story.

In those days, stories needed philosophical weight—like an ethical or moral dilemma. When I would go in to get assignments, it was helpful if I could give them the theme of the story rather than the details—like, "It's a story about mother love. Or, it's a story about betrayal." Then they would understand.

Here's another thing that was different in those days—novelty! You couldn't give them the same show they had last week. They basically wanted the same thing each week in terms of the apparatus of the show, but it had to be different in some meaningful way. In those old shows like The Streets of San Francisco, Perry Mason, The A-Team, there's always an enemy—a social fault, or a moral or ethical dilemma that needs resolving.

So, what changed? In the old days, if you wanted to get a sponsor, you had to have quality. They wouldn't buy a damn thing unless it had substance. But, now, you have more sponsors, and no sponsor is going to tell you what to do. If they don't like an episode, so what? They figure a series is likely to die after a year, anyway. They make one deal, the money changes hands, and then they're on to the next deal. I became very aware of the growing trend where sponsors had less power and control.

Also in the early days, they had Kinescope. Almost all live shows were Kinescope. But, once they started making film, that film could be recycled—and everyone knew that. That meant the film could be saved and become a rerun. Suddenly, anything that was filmed had a shelf life.

Take the old Playhouse Ninety show for the General Electric Theater, or other prestige shows. They would run once—live—and then they were gone. There was a director in a sound booth, editing and directing as he went. When live worked, it really worked, but with live production, there was the potential for accidents. Now you can get the live look without multiple cameras. When they went from three-camera shows to filmed shows, they gained a syndication market.

I always knew the shows that would have the best shelf life would be pulp—not realism. Pulp always has a special form of exaggeration. A character is not just a gunfighter, but the fastest gun in the west. A killer isn't just a murderer—he's Bluebeard. Or someone takes a ride on a comet, or voyages to another planet.

~ A Penny for Your Thoughts ~

After *Sea Change*, George's next attempt at collaboration with Rod Serling results in *A Penny for Your Thoughts*.

They were anxious to make nice and find me another story after giving Sea Change back to me. So, I started thinking...

I dreamed up this story, wrote the outline, and had a consultation with Buck Houghton. I asked him, "What about this one?"

He said, "I sort of like that one if you can work the kinks out of it."

It is the story of a very timid bank clerk who gains power to read people's minds. He is embarrassed by his ability to look in on other people's thoughts. He doesn't enjoy it, and finds it to be a startling thing. Imagine having the ability to hear the clickety-clicking of someone's mind. It's an age-old dream.

If someone really were to gain the power of telepathy, and that person were an intelligent, well-read person, it's a more likely scenario than if the person were just some guy from the woods. The more unlikely it is, the greater the power to be affected through it. If a timid bank clerk has the power to read minds and is embarrassed by it, that's a very different story than if a trained investigator has the power.

When Buck said, "We'll buy this one instead..." (as a way to make up for returning Sea Change to me), I said, "Well, no...I want the opportunity to write a first draft script." Instead of selling them stories, I was ready to sell them scripts.

On their side, they were trying to avoid that. When they bought a story from Richard Matheson or Charles Beaumont, they would buy the story and own the rights to it, and then hire Matheson or Beaumont to adapt their own stories. That sort of distanced them from the project.

I didn't realize what I was doing until months later when Buck Houghton reminded me in a subtle way that the reason I was writing scripts for the show was because I'd made him do it. At first, I turned a little cold over this, but then I realized it was just the way the business worked. He preferred to have me out there writing stories for Rod. That way, he had stories he could work on when he ran out of things. Now, I was writing actual scripts.

George sold them the story with an option to write the first-draft teleplay—an option which Buck and Rod happily exercised.

So I turned in the script, and was astonished when they loved it the way it was, and didn't want a second draft. They were ready to film it—which thrilled me!

Again, I was on set, this time with Dick York, Dan Tobin, other journeymen actors, and Cyril Delavante—a little tiny man playing Mr. Smithers, the bank clerk. I was meeting with Delavante, who was an actor who had been around since the silent films. He was such a good actor, and gave the role a great deal of heart.

So, there I was with A Penny for Your Thoughts, the first story where I actually got to write the teleplay.

George goes on to write four scripts for *The Twilight Zone*, and furnishes four stories where others write the scripts—two by Rod Serling, one by Beaumont, and one by Richard DeRoy.

~ The Prime Mover ~

When George writes his story, *The Prime Mover*, Rod Serling buys it and hires Charles Beaumont to write the teleplay. The story deals with a telekinetic man who can move objects with his mind.

The idea of a man who could read the minds of those about him is a wish fulfillment. There are many forms of wish fulfillment. For example, we've all had dreams where we could fly. Well, a man with telekinesis can turn a doorknob or control the fall of the dice—have them flip around and land the way he wants them to. He can open a drawer with his mind, have a spatula float over and finish frying his eggs. That's wish fulfillment.

I'd been wondering about this ability, and asking myself, if a man could will the drink into his hand so he didn't have to get up to get it, what would happen? If you could pull and push things with your mind, after a while, wouldn't you lose the ability to lift your arms? Wouldn't your limbs atrophy?

Those ideas for The Twilight Zone come from "the marvelous." Once I had started making sales to The Twilight Zone, I found myself deliberately thinking about the marvelous—that your dog could talk, that you meet someone who looks exactly like you, or you find you have the power to restore life.

Or, maybe money really does grow on trees. An old lady finds a strange looking bush in her backyard. She takes a magnifying glass with her out into the backyard, and when she examines the corner of one of the leaves, it's the edge of a dollar bill. She's been watering the tree with a common watering can, having no idea what was happening. She looks at another leaf—another dollar bill!—and then another!

Or, Hell really does freeze over. How could that happen? Maybe it's a result of the wind-chill factor.

Or, maybe science fiction comes about through a curse: "May your baby grow horns!" Or—as my wife remembered from her Russian Jewish childhood, "May beets grow on your ass!"

A wish that would be "marvelous" if fulfilled is what The Twilight Zone is all about. Take a genie or a flying carpet, for example. Or, consider the blue rose of forgetfulness. Now, whoever possessed that rose could give it to someone and they'd forget. The evil grand shaman in the story gives the rose to the princess so she will forget she loves this man he's conspired against. Now, he thinks he's gotten rid of him. Maybe there's some tragic thing in your life you no longer grieve, thanks to the blue rose of forgetfulness.

Consider the idea of the mask. Everyone has a forbidden desire. Imagine a mask that releases you to do that dreadful thing you don't have the nerve to do—or perhaps that heroic thing. You could be anyone under that mask of yours and no one would ever know.

There's a mask made in ancient China. Whenever someone dons the mask, the mask possesses and releases that forbidden desire. Or, a museum guard oversees a group of masks loaned by China as part of a trade from the Noh Theater. The masks had been used for centuries, and each has a label as to what it signifies. He can't resist temptation, breaks the glass, and goes home wearing one of the masks. He removes the mask, and goes into the garage where he's working on this flame thrower apparatus. The next thing we know, he's tearing through the museum, burning everything down.

Or, a policeman who usually arrests people puts on the mask and sets people free. Or, a woman who works in a beauty parlor and goes home at night to a little house in the canyon, puts a table in front of the window, puts on the mask, gets naked, and stands on the table where everyone driving by can see her. She dances naked, while listening for the traffic, and laughing as the cars crash. A detective who once possessed the mask is tracking the case.

That's surrealism's objective—to expand reality by bringing in this quality of the marvelous. It's the ability to take the imaginary and cause people to suspend disbelief so the imaginary becomes real. We all believe in this chance thing. There's one chance in a billion that you would be born the most beautiful woman in the world. You ask yourself, what if I looked like Sophia Loren? And, then you discover that you do.

If logic can accomplish the task, then it isn't marvelous. The further the distance between two disparate things, the more power it packs. We get bored with logic. It's too logical if you're in outer space and you meet an alien.

The basic Twilight Zone idea is real people with real emotions and limitations. A guy is not going to kick a gun out of the robber's hands because people don't do that—that's for superheroes. Sure, Superman can do it, but when the robber aims a pistol at someone, that's going to be one frightened and ineffective person.

The closer things are to the way things really are, the more magical the marvelous element when it comes into play. The marvelous should always be out of its element.

~ A Game of Pool ~

George's relationship with *The Twilight Zone* is flourishing, and even when his stockpile of stories runs thin, he's never short on ideas. While pitching various concepts to Buck Houghton, George floats the idea for *A Game of Pool*. This *Twilight Zone* episode will star the great Jack Klugman and the beloved Jonathan Winters. It is written as an original teleplay this time—no buying the story first.

I explained to Buck, "Look, it slows things down to have me write the outline for the story first. And on this one, a lot of it centers on the dialogue—it's the conversation that makes it interesting. It really needs to be developed into a teleplay." So, they hired me to write the teleplay.

Writing this particular story was natural for George. In Cheyenne, Wyoming, when George was only fifteen years old—and you needed to be sixteen to shoot pool in the pool halls—he learned to walk taller and carry himself with the swagger of a sixteen-year-old, in order to be allowed inside.

Going to the pool hall and shooting pool was an adult sophistication. Being able to pull it off gave me the bravado I needed to talk my mom into letting me run away from home. You see, when you're twelve years old, you walk around with great pride, certain about life. Then, puberty hits, and suddenly you feel awkward, and stop liking yourself for a while. This doesn't really settle down until you're sixteen.

To be sixteen was a mark of maturity. By strutting around as if I were sixteen, I learned to carry myself as an adult.

So, writing about pool was to write "what I know." I knew that if I were to write about a pool hall legend lecturing this younger guy, I needed to be on top of everything, and when it came to pool, I was. I knew the jargon. I understood the game. Pool is really a study in geometry.

You learn a lot about geometry by banking those balls off the side of the pool table in order to get them where they're going.

Pool is also an object lesson in dynamics. You have to know how to put spin on the cue ball to get it to stop in a certain spot or to keep it from rolling into a non-advantageous position. In my story, they talk about that a little bit: "Ah, you snookered yourself!" When you can throw in this sort of technical stuff, anyone who reads it is going to be impressed that you know what you're talking about and you have the jargon down.

So, in this story, you have a young guy challenging the champ. So, the ending is important. Who wins? The young guy—because the champ is losing power as he gets older? Or, the older guy who's still got it—because the younger guy doesn't recognize that it's all a mind game, and slips up?

Meanwhile, Charles Beaumont's book, *The Intruder* is purchased by Roger Corman with the intention of shooting the film in the bootheel of Missouri.

For the making of *The Intruder*, Corman suggests that Beaumont bring his friends along, and offers to pay for food and lodging. He is planning to have Charles Beaumont play the principal of a school.

When we got to Missouri, Bill Nolan and I helped Chuck rewrite the script so two characters became an entire motley group. Nolan and I were cast to play these racist bigots. William Shatner was wonderful as another young racist stirring up the people to resist the court order to integrate the school.

I was part of a mob resisting what were then called Negroes coming into the school system. I still remember my one and only camera direction from Roger Corman. I was in a little scene and I was supposed to have a line. I looked around to see whose turn it was to speak. Well, it was my turn but I didn't have my line. Roger slapped me on the shoulder like a football coach, and said, "Get in there, George!"

While George is on location in Missouri, *The Twilight Zone* is filming his *Game of Pool* script.

So, I'd gone on location in Missouri, and neglected to let Buck Houghton know I was leaving town. I got a call from him, wanting to know, "Where the hell are you? You're supposed to be working on the Kick the Can story!" He had given the green light on Kick the Can, and I was supposed to be there working on it—not in Missouri, making a movie.

It also came to light in that phone call that Rod Serling had rewritten the ending to A Game of Pool—my ending, which was so critical to the story! Now, instead of the old man winning the game, Rod had it so that the young man wins, and, much to his dismay, has to take up the duties of the older man.

Buck says, "It's a done deal, George. Too bad you weren't here. Now get back here with the darned script [for Kick the Can]!"

Driving back from Missouri with William F. Nolan as my passenger, we stayed in motels, where I managed to get Kick the Can largely written. That's when Bill and I became at ease with each other—comfortable enough to collaborate extensively on Logan's Run.

~ Kick the Can ~

There is George, growing in his skills as a writer, attending writers' groups and meetings to discuss all manner of things, and then going home to Lola and the kids. It is following one particular writers' group meeting where they are talking about unrelated things that his mind begins to drift back to childhood.

I find myself thinking as I am driving home, and I start considering the power of children's games. I remember friends I played with as a child—and the game we played, kick-the-can.

I start reconstructing in my head how to play the game, and trying to recall the differences between hide-and-seek and kick-the-can… Why is there a can to be kicked? What is going on there? I am only about thirty years old at the time, and yet, I cannot seem to remember the rules. That sends a chill through me.

I had only a vague and flimsy idea at that point, but I decided, I'm going to make a story out of it!

I talked to Buck Houghton about the story and the magic of children's games. Between the writing of the story and thinking about the element of the marvelous for The Twilight Zone, it hit me…what would be marvelous would be if that was how to stay young—by remembering the rules to the game! But the minute the rules of the game became too important, that's when you got old.

Buck Houghton and I both saw a story there. I had a little short story of it, and he wanted me to use that as a basis for me expanding on the idea. So, I started thinking, what is the most extreme place where the power of youth becomes important? An old folks' home! That's where our main character could come to the conclusion that, if he could only get the others to play with him, he could regain his youth.

It's a mixture of the mundane—the rest home, the situations, the people, and their concerns and fears. All that is meant to be very realistic, mundane, worldly. Yet, now comes the otherworldly element— that this could possibly be true.

~ Logan's Run ~

George's dear friend, Charles Beaumont, never gets close to old age, passing away much too early in life. George and William F. Nolan have been part of The Group, but now they are on their own, and George is at loose ends.

George and Bill have often tossed around the idea of collaborating on something, and now the idea takes on new life. Once they become free of other responsibilities and meet their other deadlines, the two began talking about the possibilities. The story that will come of their collaboration also deals with the subject of aging—and perpetual youth.

We knew we wanted to do something together, but we were not sure what. We started talking about style. We admired Alfred Bester and Ray Bradbury. We said, "Wouldn't it be great to write a book like The Stars My Destination or Bradbury's Fahrenheit 451? One of those man-against-future-technology stories."

Here's how we did it. Bill got a stack of index cards, and gave me half. We agreed to each write down character names and situations on the index cards, and in that way, we could begin working on it while we were finishing other work. Meanwhile, we would have all this ammunition in the form of code words, games, and names. Cape Canaveral renamed as Cape Steinbeck, for example, would lend a certain verisimilitude to things.

At the end, we had a pile of index cards. We looked at the words and started to brainstorm. What could "fuser" mean? A toy? A dance? A soft drink? Thick water? I'd say, "What do you think, Bill?" He'd say something like, "Well, it sounds like something commonplace but inexplicable."

The pair then sets off for the ocean breezes of Malibu, California, and rents a motel room—by the week. Their plan is to drive there together, set up a card table in the motel room, and see what they can produce.

While we were working, we made a map. We had Logan's Run as the title. Our first approach to the story was, "A Wild Gun for Morgan 3." Morgan became Logan. A gun gets loose in a future where no one's supposed to have weapons. We started thinking in those terms. It was clearly a story about man against the system.

It was all part of a pattern during which we started turning out pages—manufacturing as we went. We were taking turns at the typewriter. We had thirty-seven pages of over-written stuff. I said, "Bill, this is hopeless." But he said, "Let's finish. For God's sake, let's do that!"

So, we continued on our way, and as we did, we began to see a pattern. Chapters didn't begin with action but began with a purple passage, defined as "a piece of writing where writers are in love with the words, where things are extreme, lurid, overwritten, where exaggeration comes into play."

What do I mean by that? Words are such large boxes with words packed inside. By the time you've unpacked them, you have enough for a book.

There we were, trying to come up with new concepts as we went, thinking like Bradbury. We got a two-and-a-half-feet-by-four-feet piece of cardboard, and began to try to work with it like a game board. If he starts here, he could go to a peep party where people bring along cameras, go out onto the ribs of the three-mile complex, find stuff through the windows, and photograph it. That was the sort of thing showing up on those cards, and we would ask ourselves, how would that work? Back and forth we went with it as we tried to shape it.

On one occasion, Bill and George have been working all afternoon, and decide it is time to break for lunch. So, they go to a nearby Red Lion restaurant, overlooking the sea, and order their lunch. Gazing out the windows at the crashing waves, George has a brainstorm.

Suddenly it hit me, "What about different environments under the sea? What would be a good environment?"

We started to talk, dividing things up. "I know more about Fredericksburg and the Civil War, so I'll take that part. Why don't you do the thing about the sea?" Then, we split up on our typewriters. I wrote the intro chapters for the part dealing with whales, the undersea protein processing plant, and the earthquake that took place in the past.

The idea was that Logan and Jessica are on the run and find themselves in the undersea city of Molly. There they meet a whale. Well, I can remember writing a purple passage for that—three quarters of a page of prose. I read it to Bill, and we fought it out. The language is what makes a book come alive, and we would try to come up with new ways to describe a garment. What's the character doing, wearing, playing, thinking? All these things go to make up his life.

It was the same thing with weaponry—a gun that was an all-purpose killing machine with six chambers. It had a tangler, a ripper, nitro. It contained a special bullet called a Homer Heat Seeking bullet, which is guided by your body heat, and is always looking for 98.6 Fahrenheit.

This book became a place where we could invent our own future—an ancient future! The whole place has a tired feeling to it. You find a beat-up aluminum desk, graffiti in the hallways.

Then, we started to look at the whole business of the government telling us what to do. What if in this world we were creating, they tell us when to die? They turn people in to the Sleep Shop when they turn twenty-one to make room for the new people who are on the way. Logan chases down people who try to live past their twenty-first birthday.

It's the idea of the government being in control of your entire life. The tyrannical government oversteps, but it does so for good reasons—as a means of birth control, to help maintain a stable society.

They end up in a place called Sanctuary, which becomes legendary in the book. The entire purpose of Logan's run is to try to find Sanctuary, which is basically an allegory for a guy who switches sides—a guy who uses his experience as a policeman to avoid the police.

A mere twenty-two days later, including two weeks at the motel, and one week in Bill Nolan's garage at his parents' home, they look at each other in disbelief—a draft of the book is finished!

Once our industrious duo have a good draft of the manuscript, William F. Nolan takes it home for another week, and polishes it up. Then, he brings the finalized version to his writing partner—and George discovers that the changes made by Nolan are so seamless as to be invisible. They approach an agent, agree upon five publishers they'd like to see publish the book, and start the waiting game.

We were totally surprised when E. L. Doctorow, the author who had been hired as editor at Dial Books, caught the spirit of what we were doing. We had a well-thought-out plan, but he had his own ideas. We lamented the cover which was done in the style of pulp magazines. We were perfectly aware that we were selling pulp, but we were selling high-tech pulp, not 1930s pulp. We didn't want the creaky look of an unimaginable future, we wanted the look of a future that works too well.

We wrote the book in 1967 and in 1976—nine years later!—it made it to the big screen. Along the way, several editions of the book were issued, bearing the phrase, "Soon to be a major motion picture!"

As a strange footnote, as Bill and I were working in the garage of his mother's house, his mother came running out to the garage, yelling, "They're burning down Watts!"

There we were, writing about something we thought of as an outlandish possibility for the future—the burning of Washington—and in real time, people were firing at policemen, and shooting at cars on the Harbor Freeway. This full-blown riot, almost beyond containment, was breaking out all around us.

During the nine years that pass between the writing of Logan's Run and its appearance in theaters, George is growing, changing, and adding major TV and movie credits to his resume.

It was unfortunate that our mentor, Charles Beaumont, who had been with us all along the way, didn't live long enough to see us get our big break with a hit movie. But, I knew, and that was all that mattered. If I'd had a point to prove, I had now proven it, and nothing and no one could take that away from me.

I was a lifetime member of the Writer's Guild of America, I had a screenplay credit, I had taught courses at the university—the whole world lay ahead.

I had been convinced that writing for TV was the best way to earn money as a writer, and my best shot at being able to pay the rent. Of course, if you had a bestseller, or did a lot of writing at a penny-or-a-quarter-per-word, you could make some real money, but I could never have done that in a million years. Television was for me the Holy Grail in terms of the opportunity to be a writer.

And yet, when Bill Nolan and I speculated on our book, it eventually became a movie. With a book, there is always the opportunity to sell it to the right place and make some money.

But, television was better suited to my natural inclinations. I think of myself as a sprinter rather than a long-distance runner. I work best when I have something short to do. That way, I can really apply myself for a month or so, and then take a month off to regroup.

~ Nothing in the Dark ~

Nothing in the Dark—the story about Mr. Death and the old lady—is the most triumphant of all my accomplishments.

This is a story about an old lady who fears death. She becomes obsessed with the idea that if she can stay locked inside her room, death can't get in to get her. Then, you have a shot of this man on the doorstep.

He's so pitiful; he pleads with her. He sees that her room is all boarded up, and he says, "You haven't brought me the doctor. I need the doctor!"

She says, "But, I never go out! A boy brings groceries. I'd never go out. I fear that Mr. Death is out there!"

Redford says, "Is Mr. Death a real person like you or me? How can death be in so many places at once?" He backs away, tries to understand her strange obsession.

She lets him in. He is there to convince her that it's her time, but to do so in a fashion that won't hurt her in any way. He takes her to Heaven.

I don't know how Robert Redford ended up being cast as Mr. Death. But, now, he's this adult Mr. Redford who's had this incredible career, and by becoming important, he made that character important. You watch that episode now and you say, "Hey, wait a minute! That's Robert Redford!"

Then, you had Gladys Cooper, with her great history of refined English ladies in big dramas, or housekeepers, like in Rebecca. Together, Gladys and Robert made this show so hot, and there was also the drama of the story, itself.

I once saw a lovely Mexican film about a man running through a tavern, trying to keep a candle lit. The candle was his life, but he couldn't keep it lit. I see stories all the time, and one day, something in me synthesizes.

The story of Mr. Death and the old lady is stolen from Bradbury—but I came up with it without even knowing I was stealing from Ray. He wrote Death and the Maiden. *In his story, there's a maiden in a castle, and a young man on a spirited horse with a feather in his hat. He sees the maiden, takes out a mandolin, and sings to her in the evening. He makes himself attractive to her.*

The young man is sincere and loving. The two are struck by each other. He sings her songs and pleads with her. She leans out the window, saying, "I can't do that! My father told me if I leave the castle, I'll die."

At last, she comes down out of the castle, joins the man on the back of the horse, and rides off. We come to realize her fears were well-founded, and we come to accept death with all its beauty—death as a sincere young man, not a grizzly figure with a scythe, not a skull and crossbones.

Death was sincere. He was not out to hurt, but to soothe and calm. That idea is so profound and important to people that fear death. Death can be given a human attitude.

I wrote the script based on a simple teaser. At that time, I had enough credibility with Buck Houghton that I could just show him the teaser. He had no idea what the old lady and Mr. Death would talk about once he got inside her house. But, he gave me a shot at it, and I went home and started writing it.

I had most of it completed, typed up, and ready to turn in when Stacy McCall, a friend of mine, dropped by. He was one of the few people that felt free to do that. Stacy writes story poems. Anyway, he walked in, and we started talking. Suddenly, I realized I was not happy with the script. I left Stacy talking with Lola, and I went into my work room. I wrote six pages to replace my original opening.

It wasn't that he'd made suggestions about my story, but his excitement, the fact that he was responding to what I was doing, inspired me.

When I turned it in, they shot it, first draft. They never changed a word. Looking back, I think, so this is how good I can be?

Nothing in the Dark was a show where we got an opportunity to go on set and meet everyone. First we had a meeting.

R. G. Armstrong played the part of the building contractor that comes to the door. There are things Mr. Death can't argue for, so he shuts up, and brings in a surrogate who starts talking about the importance of dying. He isn't a destroyer—he helps them build the new things. He can talk about things Mr. Death can't. It's really a continuation of, "You didn't want to be born, either, but you have found it to be a good thing."

Gladys Cooper instinctively adopted a north country, cockney accent for her character. At first, I was like, "Oh, God, don't do that!" I saw her as the patrician lady, very powerful, elegant, well-cultured. But, as I listened to her, I realized, wait, that sounds so much more real, and so much less theatrical than the grand lady. She played the part with such conviction.

When the show first aired, she missed it. When she came back into town, the director, Lamont Johnson, showed her the episode. He later shared with me that, as she watched it, she kept repeating, "That poor woman, that poor woman." She was so absorbed in the story itself, she completely disassociated from her own performance, and was able to experience it as a spectator. It was the highest compliment she could have paid me as the writer.

Some people don't believe things can ever be perfect, but I don't see any flaw in that story. It's the best thing I've ever done.

~ Ninety Years ~
Without Slumbering

Ninety Years Without Slumbering starred Ed Wynn, the father of Keenan Wynn. He was very sensitive, and did a very good job. I thought, how fortunate to have Ed Wynn in the episode! Considering the great reverence the entertainment industry holds for Mr. Wynn, his appearance in the show already distinguishes it.

I wrote the story for Buck Houghton, and submitted it right at the time he was leaving. I had called it The Tick of Time, but when I received a copy of the script, it was now called Ninety Years Without Slumbering. If Buck Houghton had still been there, it would have been automatically understood that I'd be the one to write it. But, the teleplay came back to me half crippled.

The teleplay was written by Richard DeRoy under the instruction of William Froug, who had taken over the show. So, I didn't get on to the set while it was being made. I was out of the loop when they decided to put Richard on it. The version in my Twilight Zone Scripts and Stories book is my version.

Anyway, it was in outline form when I sold it to them and the show came out not exactly as I'd written it, but based strongly on my idea. That gave me another credit on the show. I was not greatly approving of it, but had to admit it did have emotional punch.

The idea is that this character receives a grandfather clock as a birthday present, and becomes obsessed with the idea that the clock is ticking out his life. Now, he has grown old.

There was a wonderful little lullaby, and I read the lyrics somewhere...

> *My grandfather's clock was too large for the shelf*
> *So it stood ninety years on the floor,*
> *It was taller by half than the old man himself*
> *Though it weighed not a pennyweight more.*
> *It was bought on the morn of the day that he was born,*
> *And was always his treasure and pride;*
> *But it stopped short, never to go again,*
> *When the old man died.*
> *Ninety years without slumbering,*
> *Tick, tock, tick, tock.*
> *His life seconds numbering,*
> *Tick, tock, tick, tock...*
> *~Henry Clay Work (1876)*

That song has always intrigued me. It has a certain nostalgic power.

You require some magic to get a Twilight Zone story going. The new baby is on the way. The Sullivans—Connie and Foster—are happily redecorating Grandpa's bedroom and turning it into a nursery. Meanwhile, he's being moved into the den. There is no room for his furniture anymore—his furniture, his four-poster bed, his grandfather clock.

When grandfather learns they plan to sell the clock, he reveals his odd and frightening obsession—the belief that his fate is tied up in that clock.

I started thinking, okay, this guy has got this obsession. Now his family is moving in, it's getting crowded, and they want to get rid of the clock. It takes up too much space.

Does grandfather really believe his obsession? Just look at the clock! It's a mechanical device. It's made of wheels, levers, weights.

Grandfather will stop them from selling his clock—with force, if necessary.

Connie excuses herself. It's almost time for the baby.

Grandfather tries to explain how he feels. The clock belonged to his grandfather before him. On the day he was born, grandpa died, and the clock stopped at the minute of the old man's death. Now, the clock is his. It's chiming has awakened him for work and soothed him to sleep. Through the still watches of the night, he's heard it tick, giving him strength to face each new day. How can they expect him to give it up?

But it's out of place here. It's an eyesore. It doesn't even keep accurate time! Everything gets old, and when they are old and worn out, it's time to get rid of them.

The starch seems to go out of grandfather.

Foster tries to apologize, but Grandpa is too sunk in misery.

The jeopardy comes when the clock is being moved, and the old man is trying to keep the clock moving with the help of a young boy. I liked the idea of placing the clock in jeopardy in a real setting—a small group of people saying real things while the old man's obsession is being played out.

The episode opens with Rod Serling saying something like, "A cumbersome and noisy relic of a vanished time, but this clock is unique—it keeps time in the Twilight Zone…"

It was a sweet little fable. The understanding on the part of the audience that if the clock stops ticking, the old man will die—that's the fantasy element that's always present in the Twilight Zone.

~ Identification ~

Part of my power is that I have a pretty clear picture of myself. That is to say that I can stand outside myself, look at myself, and place myself in the world. I know I'm a very plain guy in many ways. For example, I know just how ordinary my desires are or my tastes for food.

Check me out and I seem commonplace. The clearer I am thinking, the more ordinary I seem. The thing about me is, that's the impression— that I'm basically just an ordinary guy. But, when it comes to where people rank in the world, I'm a writer of popular culture.

When they asked Frank Sinatra, "What did you bring to music?" he answered, "A certain innovation in popular singing." It's so wonderful for a man to see himself realistically.

Knowing that I'm an ordinary guy, the kind of person you'd encounter on the bus, someone without exotic tastes who doesn't need a front, gives me great power. You could drop me off in Bombay—without money, job, authority, barely able to speak the language—and someone would bring me a plate of food. I could get out of calamity or endure it. I'd come through it thanks to a greater sense of power.

I have always driven myself to become a great reader. That's what makes me what I am—that business of being able to read in lieu of formal education. If you can read, you can become an educated person. Through the years, I became a better reader, and that became part of my clout.

People become bored with their own mundane thoughts of the world, and bored with themselves. They seek diversions, and one of those diversions is a book. You're getting synthetic experience in a book, but it's real. You can be that rider on the horse on the page. It's this business of identification that allows you to participate in the action, the jeopardy, the fear, the pity, whatever.

The reader has a fantastic imagination; he just needs it sparked. Give me the right couple of words and the reader rears a mountain over his head.

People would say to me, "George! How imaginative you are!" I came to realize that everyone has a fantastic imagination, but some people put their imagination to sleep.

A good writer knows that all he has to do is talk about the biting wind on the bare mesa, and the reader is transported to an old Clint Eastwood film in his mind. If you can put the reader there with a few carefully chosen words, he'll respond. Everyone knows, for example, that the Lone Ranger said, "Hi-ho, Silver!" You just have to find the words that have that quality.

The small print is filled in through the act of identification. The reader is inside a movie inside his head. As he reads, the words trigger images. The fuller his head is, the more he can bring in the details, and the better the movie he will see in his head.

Most readers don't realize the act of imagination that goes into identification. You have to be able to use your own memories and experiences to walk in my moccasins and see through my eyes.

Anyway, I'm a great reader, which allows me the opportunity to be a great writer, provided I possess the judgment to know what's worth emulating.

~ Unity ~

I am who I am because I have broken all taboos, and having broken them, I feel absolutely free. I am free to think, to do strange things, to associate with strange people. Sure, I hung out with Charles Beaumont, John Tomerlin, Jack Russell, William F. Nolan, Richard Matheson, Ray Bradbury, and many other great writers, and that was one world for me, but I have a number of worlds in which I move.

I have watched the world changing and realized I'd better get used to it. I saw the old idea of the pitch fall down. Now, you'd be in these pitch sessions, freely giving away ideas, only to discover they were later used—but perhaps not by the guy you told them to.

I watched the arrival of staff writers, where a show could recycle the work between this small group of four, five, six writers, all writing episodes of a show. When you have a handful of people rotating the writing between themselves, you end up in a situation where management is running the union.

Before those changes, it was a personality game. That's the one thing I always had going for me—my personality. I watched staff writers take over television, and watched television becoming more stylized and generic, and less inventive. But, I never allowed myself to be "shopped." Everything I did, I did without compromise.

I understood that no agent could do my act—my personality, my influence, the way one goes about things. My act is what got me my work. But, while my personality got me my work, my writing kept them coming back for more. All the personality in the world is no substitute for being able to write.

When I am writing a story, I rough-draft it, then re-think it. Now I have an ending. The ending may be great or not so great, but I have an *ending. Now, I go back and rearrange the opening so that it's congruent with the ending, and there is a feeling of unity.*

How like a story the universe is, with its many subchapters and subplots—those moving, sweeping things that historians notice later about the shape of a century, and the way it differs from the previous one or two. I think that like a story, the universe must have a peculiar beginning in order for the ending to have the dynamite it needs. So, I say, let's go back and alter the beginning so it's congruent with the ending.

I know myself to be merely a mortal man—yet, as a writer, I have been put in the position of a god. "This is going to be an incredible thing, this story. Now, let's see…how can I start the beginning… what about 'Let there be light!' Now, that's a heavy opening line."

These thoughts echo through me—thoughts about how a story could be dynamically designed so it ends with completeness and sweep, and echoes back through the work so the reader can feel like, "Ah! Of course!" So he can feel like he wrote the story himself. That's what every reader wants—to feel like he is not a reader reading, but the one who wrote the story.

Everyone wants to reach the end of a book, and think to himself, "Of course! How could it be possibly be otherwise?"

In Ninety Years Without Slumbering, the story ends with Grandfather trying to figure out how he will transport the clock safely home from the antique dealer who bought it from the family when they were selling off Grandpa's things to make room for the baby. A cab driver flatly refuses to transport it. Then the old man sees a kid on the street pulling a red wagon, and he gives the kid a dollar to help him. The antique dealer helps him load it onto the wagon upright.

The kid wants to take his wagon and go home. His mom will be looking for him!

The clock tips to one side. "Get help, kid!" the grandfather yells.

Off runs the kid. Meanwhile, the old man strains against the weight of the clock. Something sags in him, and the clock stops. Is he dead? Get the clock off of him! It's lifted and set upright. There's a grating sound from the clock, and ponderously, it begins to tick again. Simultaneously, we hear a baby's cry in a nearby hospital.

Grandfather dies as the baby is born.

Later we see the clock in a museum.

Rod Serling states, "All men's lives are measured by clocks. With each tick, a second or a minute passes and we'll never get it back. But, this we take as an article of faith—that when God closes one door, he opens another, in this world and in the Twilight Zone."

Old age has always fascinated me. I like to treat old people as very sensible. They are not addled, lost, or vacant, although the old lady who used to kick up her heels may be prim and proper now. In my own life, of course, old age presses in on me. It's not a game for sissies.

~ Afterword ~

In *A Stop at Willoughby*, a Serling-penned episode of *The Twilight Zone* (cited as perhaps Rod Serling's favorite episode from the first season of the series), a man rides the train through the snowy landscape of a winter day. This particular passenger, a certain Mr. Williams, is exhausted by the demands of life beyond the windows of the train, and drifts in and out of sleep. As he is jolted awake by the lurching and stopping of the railcar, he gazes out the windows to see a bucolic summer day, in the late Nineteenth Century, in a town called Willoughby.

Looking around him, he realizes that the very railcar in which he has been traveling is nearly deserted—and very much changed. It has taken on the appearance of a locomotive from the same bygone era that he sees out the window. As he alternates between sleep and wakefulness, he slips effortlessly between the centuries, between the two locales, and between this modern-day train and the old locomotive.

Our weary traveler recognizes in the bustling summer day beyond the train an opportunity to step into a new life. He also seems to instinctively understand that the price of admission into Willoughby is the relinquishment of his old life.

So, too, does the hero of our story recognize the sound of the ticking grandfather clock, and begin to daydream—of worlds beyond, of (to quote Serling's *Willoughby* episode) "a peaceful, restful place where a man can slow down to a walk and live his life full measure."

And, one day when he least expects it, our Fictioneer, George, will hear the sounding of the chimes of that great clock, and a familiar voice, calling, "Next stop, Willoughby!"

As I look back over my life, I've been trying to make that name or slogan, George Clayton Johnson, have power, dignity, and a certain majesty that can only come if I perfect my nature, my relationships, my habits, my life, my tropisms.

It is useful to take the long view. Were my decisions wise? As I went along and I had to choose, where did I fall down? Where did I rise up? As one ponders and thinks things out, the mind floods with so much thought.

It occurs to me lately that it's not my scripts, stories, or deeds, or the wonderful glitter of my life that is the work of art. Those pieces are samples of my aesthetic nature at play in those various fields. Those stories, it turns out, are just artifacts to prove I am an artist.

I'm very aware that the real work of art is me, myself. It's in my continual quest to shape this person into someone with more tolerance, understanding, and whatever other qualities I deem to be grand, that I find my life's meaning. And what I have found is that my only real purpose in life is to keep my wife, Lola, happy.

~ ACKNOWLEDGMENTS ~

My heartfelt appreciation to my dear friend and mentor, George Clayton Johnson, for entrusting me with your life story, and for all the love and support. You've been like a second father to me. And thank you, Lola and Paul Johnson, for eight years of patience while I finished my book on George!

My profound gratitude to Ben Ohmart, Sandy Grabman, Michelle Morgan, Valerie Thompson, and the entire BearManor Media staff for making the preparation and publication of this book such a lovely experience.

Special thanks to Billy Maddox and Billy Hammett, my friends, colleagues, and comrades around the virtual water-cooler.

Very special thanks to my faithful brother, Ray...for a lifetime of rock-solid love, especially during those long, dark years when all we had was each other.

I want to acknowledge the following people, who have helped to further my writing career: Christina Welsh and Shed Behar, for taking a chance on a neophyte with a penchant for dangling modifiers; Paddy Calistro and Brittney Ryan, for seeing in my writing something worthwhile; Wayne Orkin, for your remarkable support and generosity; Flo Selfman, for introducing me to George, and for all the great camaraderie and editing; Richard Hoffman, for great publicity and kindness.

Deepest appreciation to the following loved ones for their enduring love, support, friendship, and encouragement: My treasured friends, Jill Stein, K.D. Farris, Lesley Kyle, Christina Bowie, Nanci Wise, Alfred Medrano, Michael Barbera, Paulette Medwin, Iris Berry, the Pierres, Joan Yarfitz, Henry Fields, Jason Hughes, Bob Lancer,

Melanie Vare, Lori Bauer-Duran, and Sally Walsh; my lamplighters and fellow travelers on the spiritual path, Dr. George Cladis, Seth David, and Aimee Willis; my magical songwriting partners and soulmates, Janni Littlepage, Jimmy Waddell, and Johan Seige; Uncle Paul and Aunt Judi, cousin Melissa, my dear brother Matt, and my dear sister-in-law, Ana.

~ About the Author ~

Vivien Cooper is the daughter of the late mechanical special effects technician, Larry Needham (*Bewitched, Knight Rider, The Iron Horse, The Chase, Jaws 1, 2* and *4*, etc.) One of the highlights of her childhood was the day her dad arranged for her to spend on set with Rod Serling. Her early encounter with Rod Serling, and later friendship with George, confirmed what she has always believed—that her life is divinely guided. As fate would have it, she would get to meet many of her musical heroes, as well.

The Los Angeles native lived in Nashville from 1990 to 1997, and considers it her second home. She is an author, poet, and song lyricist, with collaborations on musical works by Janni Littlepage (*Strange Angels*), Jimmy Waddell (*Smoke Through My Fingers*), and Johan Seige. Her rhyming and rhythmic children's app, *The Instrumental Alphabet*, co-created with award-winning illustrator, Greg Carr, is available on Amazon. In her day job as a ghostwriter and developmental editor since 1999, Vivien has written and edited many published memoirs. (Watch for Vivien's second edition of *Making Hollywood Magic*, soon to be published by BearManor Media!)

She shares George's belief in a benevolent God, attends mass often, and looks for the highest good in all things. When she is not writing, listening to music, wandering around the museum, or spending time with loved ones, she can usually be found at the movies.

~ Index ~

Numbers in **bold** indicate photographs.

Ackerman, Forrest J. 100, 141
All of Us Are Dying 5, 133-134

Beaumont, Charles 21, **95**, 108, 128, 129-131, 133-134, 139-140, 141-142, 145, 149, 155, 156, 157, 162, 167, 170, 183
Bloch, Robert 141, 142, 146
Bradbury, Ray 17, 130, 133, 146, 147-148, 167, 183
Brownstein, Lola see Johnson, Lola
Brownstein, Marilyn 108, 111, 116

Colbert, Earl 123, 124-125, 126
Cooper, Gladys **99**, 173, 175
Corman, Roger 162

DeRoy, Richard 156, 177
Duke, Laura Mae (mother) 8, 9, 12, 13, 17, 23, 24, 29-30, 34, 35-36, 39, 41-42, 44-45, 47, 51, 54, 55, 63, 64, 65, 67-68, 69, 70, 73, 74, 76, 115, 161
Duncan, Ira Spurgeon (stepfather) 41-42, 44-45, 47, 51, 54-55, 59, 63-66, 69

Duncan, Judy 12, 69
Duncan, Kathleen 12, 47, 51, 59, 63, 64
Duncan, Kenneth 12, 47, 51, 59, 63, 64
Duncan, Lola Merle 12, 69

Edge of the World, The 136
Etchison, Dennis **102, 105**
Execution 5, 59, 135-137, 153

Game of Pool, A 5, 161-163

Honey West 5
Houghton, Buck 133, 136, 137, 153, 155-156, 161, 162, 163, 165, 174, 177

Icarus Montgolfier Wright 147-148
Intruder, The **95**, 129, 162

Johnson, Charles Edward (father) 8, 9, 12-13, 25, 29, 30, 35-36, 41, 42, 55, 67, 79, 174
Johnson, Jr., Charles Edward 12, 64-66, 76

Johnson, Judy **90**, 116, 123
Johnson, Lola (wife) 91, 111-113, 115, 116, 117, 118, 121, 122, 123, 125, 128, 129, 130, 133, 137, 141, 165, 174, 188
Johnson, Paul Bradford **90**, 116, 123
Johnson, Ramona Mae 12, 17, 64, 65, 69, 71, 73, 79
Johnson, Ronald Lee 12, 64, 65, 68

Kay, Gilbert 125-126
Kick the Can 5, 67, 162, 163, 165-166
Kung Fu 4, 5

Law and Mr. Jones, The 5
Lawford, Peter 125, 126, 127
Logan's Run 5, **92, 93, 94, 96, 98,** 163, 167-171

Man Trap, The 150
Matheson, Richard **105**, 130, 141, 142, 155, 183
McCall, Stacy 174
Melson, Robert 117-118
Ninety Years Without Slumbering 5, 177-179, 184
Nolan, William F. **95, 102, 103, 104,** 130, 139, 162, 163, 167, 169, 170, 183
Nothing in the Dark 5, **99, 101,** 173-175

Ocean's Eleven 5, 123-128

Penny for Your Thoughts, A 5, 7, 153, 155-156

Peterson, Charlie 16-17, 19-20, 43
Pollock, Abie 31, 43-44, 47, 49, 52, 53, 59, 60, 63
Prime Mover, The 5, 128, 157-159

Redford, Robert **101**, 173
Rogers, Bob 83, 108, 123-125
Route 66 5, 151-152
Russell, Jack 107-109, 123, 128, 183

Salmi, Albert 137
Sea Change 153, 155
Serling, Rod 1, 6, 134, 135, 136, 153, 155, 156, 157, 163, 179, 185, 187, 191
Shatner, William **95**, 162
Sinatra, Frank 57, 127-128, 181
Sohl, Jerry 133, 141, 142
Sprinkle, David 43, 68, 69
Star Trek 5, 36, 65, 149-150
Stewart, Malcolm 126
Stop at Willoughby, A 187

Tomerlin, John 130, 139, 183
Twilight Zone, The 1, 3, 4, 5, 6, 59, 60, 67, 107, 128, 130, 133, 134, 135, 141, 153, 156, 157, 158, 159, 161, 162, 165, 177, 178, 179, 185, 187

Van Vogt, A. E. 141, 146

Wells, H.G. 58, 135
Wynn, Ed 177
Wynn, Keenan 107, 177
Wynn, Jeanie 113
Wynn, Paul 113

www.ingramcontent.com/pod-product-compliance
Lightning Source LLC
Chambersburg PA
CBHW061307110426
42742CB00012BA/2091